A Stormy Epiphany

Debra Q. Rogers

© 2020 Debra Q. Rogers
A Stormy Epiphany
Kingdom Builders Publications, LLC

All rights reserved. No part of this book may be reproduced or transmitted in any form or by any means without written permission from the author.

* All Scriptures are taken from the King James Version

Printed in the USA

ISBN 978-0-578-68858-9 Soft Cover
Library of Congress Control Number : 2020908261

Authored by
Debra Q. Rogers

Editor
Louise James
Rosalind Woodruff
Kingdom Builders Publications

Cover Design
LoMar Designs

Picture for cover
Image 90359030 | Dreamstime.com

A Stormy Epiphany

This Book Belongs to

DEDICATION

This book is written in memory of my parents, the late Jacob Esau and Thelma Miriam Quillen and my grandmother, the late Rosa Grant Jackson. The ones who instilled in me every ounce of Jesus they could collect. The ones who prayed for me and my spiritual being until they could no longer pray. To God be the glory for blessing me with these guiding lights.

CONTENTS

DEDICATION..IV

ACKNOWLEDGMENT...8

INTRODUCTION..10

CHAPTER ONE...12

CHAPTER TWO...21

CHAPTER THREE 25

CHAPTER FOUR..27

CHAPTER FIVE..30

CHAPTER SIX..34

CHAPTER SEVEN 37

CHAPTER EIGHT 39

CHAPTER NINE...42

CHAPTER TEN 44

CHAPTER ELEVEN..47

CHAPTER TWELVE...51

CHAPTER THIRTEEN 53

CHAPTER FOURTEEN 56

CHAPTER FIFTEEN 59

CHAPTER SIXTEEN 63

CHAPTER SEVENTEEN 67

CHAPTER EIGHTEEN 71

CHAPTER NINETEEN	75
CHAPTER TWENTY	78
CHAPTER TWENTY-ONE	80
CHAPTER TWENTY-TWO	83
CHAPTER TWENTY-THREE	87
CHAPTER TWENTY-FOUR	90
CHAPTER TWENTY-FIVE	94
CHAPTER TWENTY-SIX	96
CHAPTER TWENTY-SEVEN	100
CHAPTER TWENTY-EIGHT	102
IN THE STILL	110
ABOUT THE AUTHOR	113

ACKNOWLEDGMENTS

My first thanks belong to God for saving a wretch like me. Thanks be to God for instilling in me the capability to transform my thoughts, trials, and test into a testimony. God is my rock and my salvation. My trust and hope is forever in my Heavenly Father.

To the love of my life & soulmate, my husband, Gordor F. Rogers, thank you for the wealth of unwavering support you have always provided. You continue to keep me grounded when I get ahead of myself. Thanks for bringing the necessary balance in my life. You are the epitome of what a husband should be. You are truly a God send. I love you to life.

To my two children; Mikeem Muldrow and Kanesha Lee, thanks for always supporting me and pushing me to accomplish my dreams. Thank you both for having so much confidence in me. You are my biggest supporters. Love you both to pieces.

To my siblings Teresa, Jacob, Maxine, and Stanley Quillen who are priceless, thank you guys for always being there and loving me even when I played the role of "momma." Thank you all for the faith and confidence you demonstrate in your baby sister's abilities to momma the clan. I love you all dearly.

To Bentley Elijah Muldrow, my only grandchild, you stole Grammy's heart. Thank you for bringing so much joy to my heart. You have opened my eyes to things previously unseen. Grammy loves you.

To my niece Shalawn; who has always had my heart, thank you for loving and supporting me and always looking up to me. To my niece Keawana; my nephews; Quantae, Trey, and Kobe, thank you all for the love and respect you always show me. I love you all!

To my Sister-in-Christ and friend Sandra "Bonnie" Hickson, thank you for so many years of being a faithful friend whom I can confide in. Thanks for always being there no matter what time of day or night. God blessed me when He connected our lives over 30 years ago. Thank you for putting up with me. Love you always.

To my Sister-in-Christ and friend; Elizabeth D. Coleman thank you for being an extended big sister and friend. Thanks most of all for your courage to tell me what I need to hear, even when I disagreed. Thanks for loving me in spite of. Love you always.

To Carol H. Hicks; my friend and former colleague, whom I thank with all my heart for sharing so much knowledge with me unselfishly. Thank you for believing in me and pushing me to reach my full potential. I knew our friendship was no accident when I realized you and my husband, your husband and I share birthdays and my grandson and your daughter share birthdays. Who could have brought us together with such commonalities but God? Love you Carol H. Hicks

Thank you to Mrs. Bernice Smith, for her love and support, and for sharing her wealth of biblical knowledge.

To Reverend and Mrs. Merritt Graves and our church family, thank you for always being the loving and supportive people you are.

Finally, I would like to extend my gratitude to Patricia Quillen who introduced me to the professionalism of Kingdom Builders Publications, LLC. The commitment and dedication they extended was unprecedented. I felt at home on my very first meeting with Mrs. Smith and the rest is history. I know I'm blessed to cross paths with Kingdom Builders Publications staff. Mrs. Smith, thanks for the work of kingdom building.

INTRODUCTION

As I meditate on the process which took this book from a dream to fruition, I am reminded of the pre-takeoff process for an airplane. Planes drive back and forth on the taxiway before moving to the runway. They are sometimes placed in a holding pattern for safety or other issues such as landing times. Once a plane is cleared for takeoff, it enters the runway. Upon entering the runway, the plane receives a thrust from the engines giving it enough force to push it forward. The composition of my manuscript was placed in a holding pattern just as aircrafts sometimes are. My holding pattern was time related. My time is not God's time and God's time is not my time. As I gleaned from previous test in my life, God allowed me to move to the taxi pattern. While I traveled back and forth on the taxiway, God groomed me for the journey. It wasn't until I stopped resisting the transformation of my test into testimonies, I received my clearance for takeoff. God's gentle nudge pushed me to share with others the peace, joy, love, assurance, and hope I received despite my shortcomings.

As a young girl, I always dreamed of writing a book. At the time, I thought I would write children's books or greeting cards. As I grew older and continued to think about writing, one day I sat down and prayed for God to give me the subject for my book. I tried writing about many different things but found myself constantly having writer's block. It was not until I wrote on the subject you are now reading that the words filled my spirit and soul. The thoughts came to me quicker than I could capture them. I started recording my thoughts until I could get to a place to write them down. God gave me confirmation and that cleared me for takeoff. God created, wrote, and illustrated my book through personal struggles, pain, disappointments, and the power HE demonstrated to turn it all around. God said He will never leave us nor forsake us, and I am a witness that He won't. I pray this book will encourage someone to keep the faith, stand on the promises of God and hold on to His hand. He will be right there with you through every storm you face. Don't lose hope!

FAITH UNDER CONSTRUCTION

Chapter One

There is a thin line between battles and blessings. February 14, 1990, was one of the happiest days of my life. God blessed me with the birth of a beautiful, healthy baby girl, the best Valentines' Day gift ever. I, was as any mother, filled with joy to have our beautiful daughter. It still amazes me how God brings life to whomever or whatever He chooses. Two weeks later, I experienced one of the most uncertain moments of my life, just the opposite of what I experienced weeks prior. In the joy and celebration of my new sweetheart, the news of her health put my faith to the test. I received confirmation that my daughter tested positive for Hemoglobin SC disease. This is a type of Sickle Cell Disease. In a matter of minutes, my life was turned upside down. It was as if I'd been dumped into a bottomless pit. I was scared, confused, angry, and anxious.

Days and weeks passed. My spirit and soul took a vacation, leaving me with an emptiness to be filled no more. I was numb. I could not feel God's presence or anyone else's. I had no desire or energy to fight. The once jovial, nothing can KEEP me down person was missing in action. All I wanted to do was ask one question after another; the question asked most often was "**Why**"?

I stayed on the *"why me"* kick for a few months. One day while watching my beautiful baby girl sleep, a voice spoke to me, "God makes no mistakes. He gave you this beautiful baby girl for a reason. Just believe." In the days to follow, I collected my thoughts, prayers, and desires so my faith could be re-directed to trust in God. I continued pondering and praying about the words spoken to me. My humanity had to be reminded of all the things I knew about God before my faith was shaken and questioned. I reminded myself God was much bigger than any devastation that could come my way and that God takes care of His own. I was told God will always be with me, even though I resigned that He was not. I was reminded when I sensed that God was no longer with me, that only signified that I removed myself from His presence.

Let us hold fast the profession of our faith without wavering; (for he is faithful that promised;)

Hebrews 10:23

God is a promise-keeper. Yes, I needed to be reminded of all these things, as we sometimes do. We wrap ourselves up in circumstances. This blocks our view of God. It's so easy to be consumed with our issues and events; doing this leaves no room for God. God is good all the time, and there is nothing we could ever do to deserve it. God is still God, having us always on His mind, even when we don't have time for Him.

My experiences taught me how to hold steadfast to God even when there was nothing tangible or emotional to hold on to. In retrospect, I realized some of the downfalls that consumed me could not win against me because God wouldn't let me go.

We ponder our decisions and plans in life we think we have a handle on, but place too much value and time in decisions on things with little to no cost. The most essential things in life which are worthy of actual value and time, we make hasty decisions about them. FAITH is one of those valuable commodities we should invest quality time and productive energy. It is not something that will develop overnight nor anything that will come by quickly, but if we are diligent and persistent in our quest to secure immovable faith, it shall come to pass. After all I agree with John Heywood on this regard, *"Rome wasn't built in a day,"* neither will your faith be.

> *Let not mercy and truth forsake thee: bind them about thy neck; write them upon the table of thine heart:* **Proverbs 3:3**

In other words, our faith begins under construction, just as the creation of a new house. You start at the ground level or phase one. As the foundation of your faith is being laid, you will find yourself seeking out a few prayer partners who don't mind hitting the floor for Jesus. Once the floor hitters are in place, you dig deeper into the word to build up the walls of faith. Once the walls are erected, you send up some timber to reach the roof of your faith. When the construction of your faith is at its highest point, there aren't any limitations on where you will be taken, if you believe. At the culmination of your faith-construction, you won't be able to contain yourself as God sends down His blessings from the windows of Heaven, so much that you will not have enough room to receive them. Yes! I tell you it is well worth the time you spend making sure your faith has been spiritually constructed. You wouldn't place much faith in a newly built home that doesn't pass inspections, why put confidence in haphazard decisions and not based on the word of God? The concept of God gives us everything we need to build our faith in His truths, His promises, and His wisdom.

> [22] *And Jesus answering saith unto them,* Have faith in God. [23] *For verily I say unto you, That whosoever shall say unto this mountain, Be thou removed, and be thou cast into the sea; and shall not doubt in his heart, but shall believe that those things which he saith shall come to pass; he shall have whatsoever he saith.* [24] *Therefore I say unto you, What things soever ye desire, when ye pray, believe that ye receive them, and ye shall have them.* **Mark 11:22-24**

> [5] *And when Jesus was entered into Capernaum, there came unto him a centurion, beseeching him,* [6] *And saying, Lord, my servant lieth at home sick of the palsy, grievously tormented.* [7] *And Jesus saith unto him, I will come and heal him.* [8] *The centurion answered and said, Lord, I am not worthy that thou shouldest come under my roof: but speak the word only, and my servant shall be healed.* [9] *For I am a man under authority, having soldiers under me: and I say to this man, Go, and he goeth; and to another, Come, and he cometh; and to my servant, Do this, and he doeth it.* [10] *When Jesus heard it, he marveled, and said to them that followed, Verily I say unto you, I have not found so great faith, no, not in Israel.*
>
> **Matt 8:5-10**

I waded through the storms that had me in a drowning state, but God threw out the lifeline. I reminisced over the times when God left me in AWE because He made the way when I saw no way. My job was to re-direct my mind to focus on Christ and not my situation. God is truly bigger than any case. My heart needed to be re-directed to the love of Christ, which strengthened me. I could feel his love and presence to love myself and others. My spirit needed redirection so I could feel God's peace and hear His voice speaking to me. Finally, I gave new directions to my life to be safely back in the arms of my Savior and give Him the praise He is so worthy of.

At that moment, I realized God was working on me, and I needed to be attentive to get this right. Who do you know would take the time to work on you, work with you, and work on your behalf when you are unworthy? Nobody but God Almighty!

> *Lord, thank you for seeing my worth even amid my unworthiness. Thank You for giving me the desire to follow Your will for my life. You are the only perfect one, and I pray I will always be reminded that You make no mistakes. Please teach me to be patient and wait for you. Help me to see that my way is not Your way. Help me to be content in all circumstances and to give you praise always. Help me, oh God, with my unbelief. I know You have a purpose and a plan for all You do, please guide me into the purpose and plan You have on my life. Make the plan clear for my eyes to see and my heart to feel. I pray in Jesus' name!*
>
> *Amen.*

November 26, 1992, Thanksgiving Day. The family was preparing dinner while reminiscing over the events which occurred over the past eleven months. Like a thief in the night, death invaded my family and took my grandmother away. This would be one of the saddest days of my life because of the sweet relationship we shared. I was selfish in that I could only think about how much I would miss our many talks and many, many days of laughter, and all the words of wisdom she shared with me in the wee hours of the night. I relinquished my selfish feeling and repeated to myself my grandmother's sufferings in her final days and how she prayed to go home to be with her Lord one day. I knew she was ready spiritually, but I was not prepared by any sense of the word. I knew she'd grown tired, so this helped me to accept what I could not change and thank God for allowing her to be a part of our earthly family for 83 years. There is no way to circumvent the pain that accompanies death, but with the love of God, you will be comforted. I thank God for praying grandmothers. This was a significant chain link breakage in my family because my grandmother was the matriarch of the family. The layers of wisdom she possessed, the domineering spirit she encamped, and her warm sense of humor brought comfort to all she came into contact with. We would now be tasked with transforming these attributes into memories. This significant loss would have me once again feeling an emptiness and a lack of focus on what would bring me comfort.

As a little girl, I listened to my grandmother talk about having faith and trusting in God. I couldn't understand why one minute she was talking, and the next moment she'd burst in a loud voice praising God as the tears ran down her face. There was no appointed time for her praise. It would happen anytime she would talk about God or even think about what He brought her and her family through. She would tell me to choose to be thankful in all things and at all times. No matter the circumstances, I want to be grateful. She reminded me that no matter how bad things appeared, there was always room for worse, and if we looked, we could find someone who would love to trade places. The time to praise God is anytime, and the location to worship Him is any place. Sincere praise comes from the heart by way of the Holy Spirit working from within, and I really got a chance to witness this in my grandmother. Don't worry about the status quo, just make sure your status is deliberate praises unto God.

I'm so grateful that God listens to the music from my heart and not my lips, for the heart is where the real music comes from. I may not be one with a melodious voice, but my praise is like sweet music to my Father's ears. The praises of my song in my spirit and soul touched me, therefore I know it touched my Father. After all, I may be witnessing to man through song, but my praises are unto God!

After the demise of my grandmother, I was once again broken, saddened, confused, and lost. I was unable to elude the feelings of loneliness and emptiness surrounding her death. I would revisit our talks, walks, rides, laughter, and late-night TV watching to bring a smile back to my face and heart. I knew I was selfish by wanting her to live longer, especially in her state of pain, but God knew I only longed for the jewel of a grandmother to bless my children as she blessed me. Through prayer, I learned again to lean on God and focus on Him and not my circumstances. I knew my grandmother was going to a better place, and I no longer worried about her pain. I will always remember the teachings, singing, and most of all, the prayers my grandmother blessed her family with. I thank God for my grandmother, Rosa Grant Jackson, who deposited an indelible impression on the banks of my heart forever.

Father, thank You for your gift of praying grandmothers who took the time to construct the faith of others. Thank You, especially for my grandmother, who took the time to teach me all about You. Bless grandmothers everywhere who understand that it still takes a village to raise a child. Bless them with Godly wisdom to instill that which is of You into the hearts of those they encounter. Keep them in your care and lead them in the way of righteousness. This and all the blessings I ask in your precious name. Amen.

September 5, 1996, the death angel would once again invade my family, taking away my daddy. Losing my daddy was very hard, given the fact that my mother's health was in a fast-declining state. I knew the passing of my daddy would be difficult for her, and all my strength was gone, and I would be of no help to her. God stepped in and showed me that it was not about my mother's power, nor mine, but about the strength that comes from Him. He would once again move to show His love and kindness toward us.

The Lord is nigh unto them that are of a broken heart; and saveth such as be of a contrite spirit. **Psalm 34:18**

I can do all things through Christ which strengtheneth me.
Philippians 4:13

My mother was a woman of great character, wisdom, and virtue. She knew that the Lord giveth and the Lord taketh away. She realized that this place called Earth was just a pitstop on the way to her eternal home. My mother also knew what **Psalms 118:14** *The Lord is my strength and my song; he has become my salvation.* Then as any Godly mother would do, she remembered **Ephesians 3:16** *16 That he would grant you, according to the riches of his glory, to be strengthened with might by his Spirit in the inner man.*

My mother never ceased to pray for her family because she understood the power of prayer. Through the passing of my daddy, I embraced the meaning of the lyrics of this old song, *"The Leaning Tree is not always the first to fall."* It was true to me because Mother was in the leaning state longer than daddy, but to our astonishment, our daddy was first to fall. We were so focused and caught up in my mother's ill state that my daddy slipped away right before our eyes. This proves that no one other than God really knows the time nor the hour that death may come. He knows the time to be born and the time to die.

April 27, 1997, three weeks after my mother's sixty-first birthday and seven months after the passing of my daddy, my mother became weaker and was hospitalized. There was nothing to be said or done to convince me that my mother would not return home. After a weeklong stay, which seemed like a month, my mother was called from a life of labor to her eternal rest. The feelings on that very day were indescribable. I knew I must be strong for my kids and siblings, but my strength was depleting. I lost three of the closest people to me: my grandmother, daddy, and mother. I was numb and empty inside, wanting to be filled with something. Something within me was broken, and I had no idea how to fix it. There were times after the funeral when I didn't know how I would make it. I had nothing to work with. I did not know where to begin to pick up the pieces nor how to put them together again. All my get up and go, got up and left. I went through the motions, but not making very much progress. To put it simply, I was going nowhere fast. I used every excuse I could to avoid facing my situation or anyone else. I chose to take a detour every time I saw reality traveling in my direction. Attending church without my grandmother, and now without my mother was a hard pill to swallow. I attended church with them for so long that it was difficult to participate without them. Where would I turn? Nevertheless, I continued attending church because it was what I needed, and I knew this was where they would want me to be.

THE AWAKENING

Chapter Two

Months later, one Sunday morning, as I watched the Bobby Jones show while getting ready for church, I cried and screamed out to God while listening to the song *The Battle is Not Yours, It's the Lord's*. I needed to lean on God while praying for strength battling the death of my precious loved ones. Have you ever been where you didn't even have the strength to pray? This was where I was at this point. My heart was willing, but my mind and soul just could not find the strength to reach my heart. This is when God lifted the prayers from my heart and wiped my tears away. He came to my rescue. His love saved and sustained my heart and soul.

God was there to dry my tears and hold me during the time when I didn't know how to call on Him. At that very moment, I gave up the fight and turned it all over to God. I made a choice to let go of the hurt and gave it to God. I let go of the fear, the emptiness, and the sorrow that consumed my life. The burdens that were lifted at that moment we insurmountable. Instead of asking God for at least half the faith and wisdom my grandmother and mother possessed, I realized I needed to pray for a double portion of what they exuded. I needed to think as Elisha thought when he asked for a double portion of Elijah's spirit. As parents, we all want our kids to do better than we have done.

I'm sure my grandmother and mother would want me to have a relationship with Christ twice as intimate as they experienced. I was now in quiet, humble praise unto the Lord, just Jesus and me. Praising him for not leaving me alone, praising him for having the patience to wait for me when I hadn't put my total trust in Him. Praising him for lovingly taking me under his wings and being the grandmother, Daddy, and Mother to me that I longed for. It was in the most raging hours that I had an "EPIPHANY," right in the middle of my storm. God was there all the time, when I seemed lonely, discouraged, lost, empty, and even when I couldn't pray. I couldn't feel God's presence because I was still dwelling on my grandmother, daddy & mother's relationships with God.

I was living as if my God died along with my loved ones. God is very much alive and well, waiting to be all I needed to get through this time of sorrow. I was my own worst hindrance. I failed to recognize what I was left with by those who loved me. I was underestimating the relationship that I developed with God over the years as I watched my parents and grandparents. The epiphany changed my whole life. It changed the way I viewed God, received God, worshipped God, but most of all, it changed the way I loved God. The most significant value was the revelation of my God-given purpose for life. God utilized the events of death in my life to build my strength in Him. He knew the purpose-designed just for me. I prayed so many years for a definitive answer for purpose in my life. When I least expected it, GOD answered my prayer. God confirmed to me that I was already living my purpose, but hadn't claimed it.

My purpose is to motivate and encourage someone every day with a kind word or thoughtful deed. A light went off in my head on that day, and since then, I've claimed my purpose. My life took on new meaning. God extended a three-fold blessing to me during this storm. In the first-fold, He took hold of me before the storm could completely consume me. Secondly, He revealed to me my purpose in life, leaving no doubt. Thirdly, He moved in my heart and led me to a serene place of healing. God breathed some good stuff in the valley of my pain. The years and years of praying to

God for my purpose in life finally paid off. This is a testament of how faithful God is and how He answers prayer in His time, not ours. This message is to anyone who has been in prayer about something for a long time, don't give up.

God knew what it would take to get me equipped to work my purpose, so much so that He allowed me to write this book as a snapshot of my purpose. Out of all the matters I've written, none of them can compare to what God has given me post my epiphany. My mission is being fulfilled every day with what God gave me. Thank God for the gift, the faith, and entrusting me with it. God puts the initiation stamp on to get things started in our lives because He is the only one who knows when we are ready to handle the purpose with our name on it.

During my storms, I allowed my fears to overwhelm me. My spiritual vision blurred in process. The *light* came on in my head with a news flash reading, "Who are you serving?" During my worst storm, God spoke to my winds of despair, and they cease to blow. He talked to my rain of sorrows, and they dissipated. He spoke to my waves of heartache, and my heart calmed. He spoke to my hail of grieve and comforted my soul. The feeling came over me that morning was the spirit of God because no one or nothing else could move me that way. No one else truly knew how desperately I needed to be rescued. I kept it from my family as much as possible because they all considered me the strong one. I never wanted to disappoint my family. They all mean the world to me. I'm glad we can't choose our families because God does a much better job at it than we could ever do. Thank God for the loving and supportive family that He blessed me with.

God knew how much my grandmother, daddy, and mother loved and trusted him. He was waiting for me to display how much love and trust I had for Him. I was so caught up in my sorrows that I failed to allow my broken spirit to be fed by the

Holy Spirit from the God I neglected. I knew my grandmother, daddy, and mother knew who God was and what He was capable of, but I needed to show God that I knew Him for myself and not just what I saw and heard from loved ones. I needed to see Him through my own eyes; not just through the eyes of those who taught me. God reminded me He would take care of me just as He took care of my loved ones. I realized as God spoke to my heart that day, it assured me everything would be ok. I had to let go and let God. Everything I encountered up to this moment prepared me for when I would let go and let God. During the worst of my storms, I finally realized God worked in my life. I was oblivious to the teachings until this moment. It finally hit me. All my mother and grandmother gave me, and the times they prayed for me were all still with me. I learned how to live with them in my heart.

LET'S GET ACQUAINTED

Chapter Three

Life has a way of knocking us off track. It behooves us to get acquainted with someone who is experienced in track replacement. No one can place us where God wants us to be other than God. I searched for a peace that I could not find, but later I learned the peace I needed was there all the time. I learned to tap in to the peace God planted in the hollow of my heart and soul when I needed a friend. I learned how to lean on my faith when my way grew dark.

The amazing blessings we receive from God are because of His goodness, not because we are good. There is nothing we can do to earn these blessings, and no one can take the benefits of God from us. What God has for us is for us. God extends these blessings to us because of the magnitude of His mercy and grace toward us. We go through daily ventures attempting to earn the approval of God and His salvation, but we will never earn salvation through good deeds. We administer good deeds because we love the Lord, and our love for Him gives us the desire to perform good acts. Our amazing God works in us through trials and tribulations to reveal our flaws. He alone can get the glory for the miraculous things He does to put us where we need to be.

> *Father God, You are my source for all my needs. Thank You for pouring into my heart and soul the love and kindness that I need to make it through each day. Thank You for not erasing my future because of my past. Help me to give You all the praise, honor, and glory that You deserve. Help me refrain from working under my assumptions and remind me to seek understanding from you in all that I do. I pray in the precious name of Jesus Christ.*
> *Amen.*

One of the most challenging things is facing the uncertainty of whether our faith will prevail during our most challenging events in life. We all would like to know beyond a shadow of a doubt that our faith will not fail us. I must admit I did not understand when my grandmother used to say, "Just keep the faith, and everything will be alright, no matter how it turns out." I lived long enough and grew spiritually sufficient to know she prepared me for when things turned out the way I prayed they would, but even more, for the times when things didn't turn out in favor of my prayers. She taught me to believe things work the way God intends for them to work, and when it is different from what we think, we should refocus our thoughts. In doing this, she also taught me even when things didn't go the way I prayed, God was still with me and always in control. That was enough to know the end results would be all good. That was just God doing what God does, taking control.

BURNING DESIRE

Chapter Four

There were points in life where I continued longing for something. No matter what I accomplished or what I overcame, it was still something missing. I had a nagging void that I just couldn't satisfy. It grew more and more enormous with the passing of each day. I wanted to grab hold of something, but I was unable to figure out what that something was. One day when I least expected it, the Spirit spoke to me saying, "You have what you need, tap into it, and lose the fear." What I heard was, I needed a little more Jesus. What I'd been working with was no longer enough. I needed to spend more time with Him to hear from Him. I needed to meditate on His word more so I would have the word in my heart in times of despair. I needed to serve Him more so He would be pleased with my living. I needed to praise Him more so He would be glorified. Yes, I needed to up my spiritual game so my relationship with God would be more intimate.

Jesus is the answer to everything we need. It is up to each of us to make the choice to trust and obey Him. There is nothing too much for our Heavenly Father to handle. Give it all to Him, and He will give you all that you need to get through any situation. There aren't any substitutes for the Holy Spirit left as the Comforter. We look for comfort in all the wrong places, only to find that there is but one true comforter.

But the Comforter, which is the Holy Ghost, whom the Father will send in my name, he shall teach you all things, and bring all things to your remembrance, whatsoever I have said unto you. **John 14: 26**

There are times when we experience uncomfortable rest, but just know that through it all, God is right there with us. He promises to never leave us, so He is there through the good, the bad, and the indifferent. He can change any situation at any time, we must continue to believe in His power to deliver us. In times when we experience disappointment in the lowest of valleys, and are fighting against the highest mountains of delays, just hold onto God's unchanging hands. It's at these times that God works to cultivate the soil of the hearts, souls, and minds of his children. Never give up on yourself, but most of all, never give up on God and what He is trying to reveal to you. Stay the course, pray earnestly, and God will lead you into the destiny that He has laid out for you. No matter how long the journey may appear to be, keep your eyes focused on the navigator, Jesus the Christ. You will reach your destination and have no regrets.

While in the valley, God talks to us, while climbing the mountain, God walks with us, even when we are not listening. What a mighty God we serve! God allows us the time and space to hear from Him. There is no joy to compare to the pleasure of hearing from God. Don't let the desire for your relationship with God grow cold.

> *13 Wherefore gird up the loins of your mind, be sober, and hope to the end for the grace that is to be brought unto you at the revelation of Jesus Christ; 14 As obedient children, not fashioning yourselves according to the former lusts in your ignorance: 15 But as he which hath called you is holy, so be ye holy in all manner of conversation; 16 Because it is written, Be ye holy; for I am holy.*
> **I Peter 1: 13-16**

> *Oh, God, our everlasting and present help, thank You for always being there for us. Thank You for not casting us away with our sins. I pray that You will continue to ignite our spirits so that we can be on fire for You. Help us to be intentional about listening for your voice. Touch our minds and hearts that we will always feel your presence. Let us not be scarce with our praises. You are an awesome God who is so worthy of all our blessings. In your name, we pray and ask it all. Amen.*

SELF-ENTRAPMENT

Chapter Five

There are some things in life that we may not have any control over, but the choices we make are not one of them. We do have control over the choices we make when we are in the deciding process. To make the decision for whom we will serve is a blessing we should cherish. We are privileged with the opportunity to worship and praise God at any time we choose, day or night. The things that we take for granted, such as freedom of choice is the freedom that others who are not so blessed, would love to have. Our passion for an intimate relationship with Jesus Christ should not be so shallow that we are unable to feel the love and presence of God in our lives. Although on public platforms, I consider myself to be a woman of few words, the opposite when it's just Jesus and me. I am a very talkative individual when my Heavenly Father is on the receiving end. I have absolutely no problem talking to Him.

Just Jesus and me, whenever I need a friend, I can count on Him. He is a friend that you can confide in with every fiber of your being. He won't turn on you, betray your trust, stop loving you, get tired of hearing from you, never too busy for you, and most of all, He is always the same. You can depend on Him to listen to you, you can rely on Him to counsel you, He will dry up your tears, and He will wash away every one of your sins.

One day while sitting and moping over something that I knew I could have done better, my grandson came to me with the curious personality and asked: "Grammy, what's wrong?" I responded, telling him I was upset because I did not do well on an exam for school. He looked at me and gave me a hug and said: "Grammy, it's ok, just do what I do when I mess up in school, erase where you messed up and start over again." Although the answer for me was not that simple, it gave me a chuckle and took me away from feeling sorry for myself and forced me to re-evaluate my priorities. The most important thing that my grandson did for me was to remind me of how God erases all of our mess ups (our sins) and remembers them no more. He gives us a new start like the one my grandson, Bentley spoke of. I am a firm believer that God can use anyone to get a message through to us. On this day, God used my grandson to get my attention so I could hear from Him. Sometimes God has to remind us to get our priorities in check. For me, this was one of those times.

God made us, and He knows us and what we need before we even realize we need anything. He knows us by name, and He wants us to get to know Him as intimately as He knows us. He delights in seeing His children acknowledge their weaknesses and turn to Him, trusting in His power to lift them above their circumstances. That's just how great our Heavenly Father is!

When you fall in love, you want so badly to please that person, well falling in love with Jesus can't compare to any other love. Falling in love with Jesus was the best thing that's ever happened to me. The urge to please Him is far more than that of anyone else. As a youth, I wanted to please my parents because of the sacrifices made and love they rendered to me. Who loves me more than God, and who made more sacrifices for me than God? He sacrificed His sinless Son to pay for the sins of the world. That's Love! Now that I am an adult, I realize there is nothing more important than pleasing God. It behooves us to get the story straight and not get hooked on what the world says about anything, but get caught on what the word of God says about EVERYTHING! The Bible should be handled as the precious cargo it is. It should be dealt with the kind of love it is meant to spread. The world we live in is full of confusion, and we must circumvent the possibilities of becoming a part of any disillusions concerning the love of God. God's love for us is all the Bible says it is.

> *The Lord is my shepherd; I shall not want.*
> *[2] He maketh me to lie down in green pastures: he leadeth me beside the still waters.*
> *[3] He restoreth my soul: he leadeth me in the paths of righteousness for his name's sake.*
> *[4] Yea, though I walk through the valley of the shadow of death, I will fear no evil: for thou art with me; thy rod and thy staff they comfort me.*
> *[5] Thou preparest a table before me in the presence of mine enemies: thou anointest my head with oil; my cup runneth over.*
> *[6] Surely goodness and mercy shall follow me all the days of my life: and I will dwell in the house of the Lord forever.*

Psalm 23:1-6

God is the source of my strength, and I shall not be moved from this space I have been blessed to be placed upon. God wants to be Shepherd, give Him your all, and watch God at work in your life. When you sense that you are trapped by disappointments, and you find the grass is less than greener on the other side of the fence, hold on and turn it over to God. He will make it right.

> *Father, thank You for watching over us both day and night. Thank You for protecting us from the dangers we see and those we have no knowledge of. Help us to be more persistent in our prayers to You and more intentional in our service to You and Your people. Help us serve You with our whole hearts and stay on the battlefield fighting for those who are unable to fight. These and all the blessings we ask in Your precious name. Amen.*

DYING TO LIVE
Chapter Six

Have you ever been so excited about something that it was hard to be contained? Have you ever felt this way and could not put your finger on the initiator of these emotions? We live a significant portion of our lives, evaluating what makes us happy, sad, worried, or relaxed. We also twist our way through life, spinning out of control, trying to figure out which path we should embark upon only to find ourselves on the wrong path. We often take several different routes before we finally realize the roads we are traveling lead to dead ends. These are one-way roads which lead to terms of destruction. This is an example of how life is without God! Life without God can only lead to a dead-end, an end of self-destruction. Any road you chose outside of the will of God, will eventually lead you to the crossroads of a dead-end. Trust me, I am a witness. Your life is before you, and it appears bits and pieces are carved away from the core. You get a close look at the big picture in totality and ask yourself what's missing? Traveling down the cross-roads of destruction can be devastating. Soon, you will be greeted with a wakeup call to your desire to live and not die. You will experience an uncanny notion to fill a void in your life that, until now, was unrecognized. It's not until you succumb to the will of God you will truly begin to live. If you thought you were living before your life with God, just wait until you start your new journey. There is nothing more rewarding than knowing you have a personal relationship with God and to know He cares for your every need.

It never ceases to amaze me when God brings me out

over and over again, despite my shortcomings. What a mighty GOD we serve! Start your new life by getting to know yourself from the inside out. Encourage yourself daily with what God gives you; this will keep you looking forward to encouragement from God. You won't be able to help the urge to inspire others. God made each of us in His own image, so he knows each of us intently. We must learn to be who we are in Christ Jesus. Then and only then will we be able to follow the plans God has purposed for our lives. You will never fulfill the purpose God has for you if you are trying to be someone else. You must learn to be content in your circumstances regardless of how bleak they may appear. Practice praising God in all things, no matter how dim the lights may be. Some of God's best work is done when we are in our darkest places. The greatest humility comes up from our lowest drops. God's powerful light shines brightest when He lifts us from our most bleak points in life. These times teaches us there are no places too dark for God to lighten. We will begin to see the peace at the end of our storms. We will display love, where love did not abide. We will find encouragement where discouragement once dwelled. We will find peace where confusion once ruled. Whenever you find yourself dying to live a life of blessed assurances, grab a hold to the promises of God, and be revived.

15 Love not the world, neither the things that are in the world. If any man love the world, the love of the Father is not in him. 16 For all that is in the world, the lust of the flesh, and the lust of the eyes, and the pride of life, is not of the Father, but is of the world. 17 And the world passeth away, and the lust thereof: but he that doeth the will of God abideth for ever. **1 John 2:15-17**

> Father, I stretch my hands to thee, no other help I know. I come to You with thanksgiving in my heart. Thanking You for blessing me beyond measure. I can't possibly thank You enough for all that you have given to me. I pray that You will touch Your children with a finger of love and give each of us a measure of faith no less than the size of a mustard seed. Fill us with Your love and let us empty on those that we encounter. This and all other blessings, we ask it all in Your precious name.
> *Amen.*

A Stormy Epiphany

THE PACE OF FAITH

Chapter Seven

Life is full of things we set our hearts, minds, and time on accomplishing and accumulating. We go as far as establishing a timeline for how and when we want something to happen. There are some things in life this approach may work for, but becoming a faithful, diligent, humble child of God is not one of those things. It takes time, patience, and practice, yes, practice! If you never exercise your faith by putting it into action, how will you ever know if you genuinely have faith in anything? Faith that fails to get a workout becomes stagnant; it becomes extra weight with no real value. The more we practice our faith, the more it becomes a part of our life, and the more effective it will become. The more your faith gets worked out, the more it shapes up with the word of God. It will become a vital part of your identity. It will become who you are, and it will become automatic to believe in the one who keeps every promise. Your faith becomes healthier and stronger whenever you fuel it with perseverance and humility.

The key to living life through our faith is not believing in the things we see but having faith in those things unseen. Take the wind, for instance, we know what the wind is capable of and what it feels like; we believe in it because God created it. We've never seen the wind; however, we have established a belief in it. How is it we find it hard to believe in the one who created the wind? How much more are we able to feel the presence of God through His Holy Spirit moving within us? Get to know your pace in the race to a stronger faith and stick to what moves you from one degree of grace to the next. All good things come from God, but it's all in

His time. Be patient and don't give up, keep pushing toward the mark. What will it take to remove our unbelief?

I have grown to be a firm believer that things happen in life when they are supposed to happen. If we were in control of when things were to happen and how they were to happen, then there would be no need for God. None of us wants to know what that looks like. We are to pray and wait as God moves on our behalf. After all, He is the one who has everything under control. He is the only one who can size up the exact pace for His children to move from one level of grace to the next. Only God knows when we are ready to handle the next level in our lives.

36 For ye have need of patience, that, after ye have done the will of God, ye might receive the promise. **Hebrews: 10:36**

If we keep the faith and live according to what God has commanded, every promise is ours in the Bible. We have an option to choose the best thing going, and the price has been paid in full.

Lord create in me a clean heart and a spirit that only want to do what is right. Lead me, guide me, and, most of all, speak to me so that I will be in a position to hear Your voice, let my light so shine so that it points others back to You. Thank You for always being my guiding light and for protecting me from the dangers that I've seen and those I never knew existed. Thank You for Your grace and mercy. In Jesus' name, I pray. Amen.

DEFEATING THE ENEMY

Chapter Eight

Life is full of ups and downs, the ins and outs, and do's and dont's. It is a task to evaluate which way to go and what actions to take to get to a resolution. The trials, tribulations, and circumstances that so easily beset us are not to keep us down, but they come to lift us up. They come to lift us up to a higher degree of grace with our Heavenly Father. Concerning the enemy, the biggest misconception to overcome is the belief that an individual is our enemy. The individual is not our enemy, Satan, who is in control of them, is our enemy. We must read, meditate, and consume the word of God which teaches us what is found in this scripture:

> *The thief does not come except to steal, and to kill, and to destroy. I have come that they may have life and that they may have it more abundantly.*
> **John 10:10**

We must shift our thought processes and learn how to pray for our enemies. No one said it would be easy, but it's not impossible. The Bible tells us all things are possible with God if you believe. It won't hurt to take a self-inventory to make sure we aren't carrying around our biggest enemy (self). We often find fault in everyone and everything, but if the truth was ever told, we would be named as our own biggest enemy. Prayer is the best answer for the enemies in our lives. Our enemy may be an addiction of some sort, it may be overextending ourselves or resources, it may be lack of consistent prayer life, it may be insufficient patience, or it may be lack of faith. Whatever personal enemies you find yourself dealing with, take them to God in prayer. There is no enemy God can't defeat. God will fight for you because He loves you and wants to see you overcome your enemies. He said in His word He will make your enemies your footstool.

> *12 For we wrestle not against flesh and blood, but against principalities, against powers, against the rulers of the darkness of this world, against spiritual wickedness in high places. 13 Wherefore take unto you the whole armour of God, that ye may be able to withstand in the evil day, and having done all, to stand. 14 Stand therefore, having your loins girt about with truth, and having on the breastplate of righteousness; 15 And your feet shod with the preparation of the gospel of peace; 16 Above all, taking the shield of faith, wherewith ye shall be able to quench all the fiery darts of the wicked. 17 And take the helmet of salvation, and the sword of the Spirit, which is the word of God: 18 Praying always with all prayer and supplication in the Spirit, and watching thereunto with all perseverance and supplication for all saints;*
> **Ephesians 6:12-18**

Each day I am blessed to be awakened by the finger of love from God, I begin with thanksgiving to God for another day, and secondly, I ask God for a measure of grace to get me through a productive day. There is no better way to begin the day than to welcome in the joy of the Lord. God's grace and mercy are sufficient for me, and I can't thank Him enough for who He is in my life. He thought enough of each of us to leave us with a comforter, accept what the comforter has to offer. Work out through your circumstances, situations, tribulations, or whatever comes your way, exercising the power of the Holy Spirit which lives in you. Allow the Holy Spirit to breathe peace into your situation and speak victory into your circumstances. Jesus promises He will be with us all the way. I believe it! No matter how many times you have been defeated by man, it's never too late to become a winner with God. Join the G Team, He has the only undefeated team.

> *Father God, thank You for leaving a comforter in the Holy Spirit to keep me in times of need. Thank You for knowing my every need and for showing so much care for your children. Help me to always tap into the Holy Spirit to soothe my soul when my ways seem dark. Because of your divine spirit, I can hold on and not be alone. Thank You for blessing a sinner such as I. We are all sinners saved by your grace, and we are ever so grateful that you continue to show your love for us. I ask for your continual blessings of fantastic beauty and let me not forget to always give you praise. I pray in Jesus' name. Amen.*

GROOMING GRACEFULLY
Chapter Nine

We all have an opportunity to come before God with grace and thanksgiving. All we have and all we hope to be begins and ends with God. Living within the grace of God is a choice we each must make at some point in our lives. Gather your thoughts and options and decide sooner rather than later, which you will choose, to favor grace or not? God is no respect of the person; He loves and cares for all of us, even with our flaws, but He is a respecter of faith and action. Sometimes the humanity in us prevents us from asking for forgiveness for our wrongdoings. Our Heavenly Father understands when we are weak, and without faith, we can't please Him, so he forgives us repeatedly and does it with a heart of compassion. How much more does he expect us to display this type of love and forgiveness for others? Jesus humbled Himself and became one of us to save us. What is too much to give for the gift of His saving grace? We are called to live a life streamed with humility.

As we live and grow in grace and humility, we should have the propensity to put others before ourselves and to be quick to ask for forgiveness. The lower we are willing to place ourselves, the more God will build us up. The lower we humble ourselves, the higher God will raise us up. Try being the initiator of humbleness and allow God to be the initiator of elevation. If you humble yourself unto God, He will elevate you unto man. This allows us to place ourselves where God can use us. The bumps and bruises we suffer throughout our growing pains will serve as reminders of where God has brought us from. I have made lots of mistakes in my life, but it was not a mistake when I pondered over the advice and words of wisdom I received from my mother and grandmother. It was those tidbits which gave me the courage to get back up when I fell. It was those words of the wise which taught me to glean from the lessons of my mistakes. I am so grateful to God for NOT giving me what I deserve; His grace, mercy, and love shields me from that experience. God doesn't intend for us to stumble our way through life. He has given us everything we need to walk through life with confidence and faith in His power and promises. Use every opportunity to groom the spirit, soul, and hope with God's grace inspired love.

2 Then make my joy complete by being like-minded, having the same love, being one in spirit and of one mind. 3 Do nothing out of selfish ambition or vain conceit. Rather, in humility value others above yourselves, 4 not looking to your own interests but each of you to the interests of the others. 5 In your relationships with one another, have the same mindset as Christ Jesus:
Philippians 2: 2-5

Lord, thank You for taking the time to groom me with your grace. Thank You for seeing something in me that was worthwhile fighting for. Please keep me working in service to you and your people. Help me to seek You in all that I do. Bless those who are actively seeking your face and touch them with Your loving hands. In Jesus' name, I pray. Amen

WHY AM I IN THIS PLACE?
Chapter Ten

Often life will take us to some places leaving us scratching our heads, wondering why or how we end up there. It is those times when we have an opportunity to take a self-inventory to evaluate how our lives line up with the will of God. The more we meditate on God's word and put it into play, the more we will examine our lives when trials come. The fact our lives are lined up with the will of God does not exempt us from tests; it just helps us to react to our situations prayerfully and from a spiritual point of view. Otherwise, our humanistic instincts kick in and take us to places we prefer not to go. We find ourselves making matters worse. We build our faith and trust upon the immovable rock to avoid being taken out of our character when trials and tribulations come. The advantage in knowing God and having a personal relationship is He ensures us this too shall pass with Him on our side. I must agree with the song, "I'd rather have Jesus than silver or gold."

God allows us to be placed in spaces that will position us to receive His grace and mercy. We must learn to work the place or the area we are positioned in until our change comes. These places are merely resting stops on our journey to a better place God has designated for us. The place on your job, in your family, in your church, or in your community; God equips us for the journey through every trial we face making us more durable for the final space. God doesn't send us straight to where He wants us to be, we must experience some things along the way to help us grow and remember we will always need Him. God wants us to receive His blessings, but the more we resist the rest stops of disappointment, time, qualified or overqualified, there's no room, why me, the longer you delay receiving the blessings God has for you. One of my rest stops was previous employment, where I was mentally abused for no reason. I did not understand at the time why I was being subject to such harsh treatment. I found myself asking over and over again, "why am I here, and how did I get here"? Little did I know, God was preparing me for something greater. God took me from the worst job of my life where I received absolutely no respect and placed me on the best job of my life, where I gain more respect than I could have ever fathomed. No one could take me from one such extreme to another but God. He moved me in His time and in His way. God will allow some bruising to take place sometimes before He can use us. We must remove ourselves and make room for Him. Anything you find in the way, move it over. God sometimes leaves you in a broken state until you can weather the therapy of rehabilitation. We may require a mind rehabilitation, soul rehabilitation, or spirit rehabilitation. Whatever the need is, God can fulfill it.

Some things must be removed before God will enter your space. No matter what is taking up the space God should be occupying, just move it over. If it's anger, move it over, if it's disobedience, move it over, if it's selfishness, move it over, if it's hatred, move it over, if it's unforgiveness, move it over. When your space is renovated and becomes filled with grace, mercy, and love, God will move in. Use your area wisely to minister to others and gain strength for your soul.

God will elevate you to higher places when He sees how you handle the cramped spaces. When you find yourself in the valley, continue to pray because God is there. If you find yourself in bondage, cry out to God because He will hear your prayer and deliver you. When you find yourself climbing the rough side of the mountain, praise God, and He will give you the strength to rise. If you find yourself falling behind on your responsibilities, lean on God, and He will pick you up and place you back on track. When you find yourself trapped in the den of failures, God will rescue you. Let nothing or no one turn you away from the path God has placed you on. The place you're in may not be ideal but get used to God's immutable power to make great decisions. Believe with all of your heart that the best is yet to come.

12 I know both how to be abased, and I know how to abound: every where and in all things I am instructed both to be full and to be hungry, both to abound and to suffer need.
13 I can do all things through Christ which strengtheneth me.
Philippians 4:12-13

Lord, thank You for being my guiding light. Thank You for not thinking it robbery to take the time to guide and direct a sinner such as I. Please order my steps so that they may always be in line with Your path for my life. Help me to see clearly the way that You have purposed for my life. Instill in me the desire to follow Your vision for my life and make the vision clear. Thank You for allowing me to be a vessel for You on this place called Earth. Keep me on track to complete your plan for me and continue to strengthen me for the task. In Jesus' name, I pray. Amen.

BALANCING THE BLESSINGS

Chapter Eleven

God blesses us in so many ways we lose count. He bestows an infinite number of blessings on every one of His children as he sees fit to do so. The way we give thanks to God for all the undeserving benefits we receive is by honoring Him. We praise God when we use what He blesses us with to bless others. He expects us to bless those who are in the greatest need. The blessings are not for us to selfishly keep for our own pleasure without sharing with those less fortunate. We also honor God when we keep His commandments and spread the good news about the Savior. There are situations we experience in life which brings a certain amount of uncomfortableness, but this is just to keep us from becoming complacent in our praises to God.

God blesses us more than enough to keep new praises on our lips. God only wants the best for us, and He uses every opportunity to bring us to the place where we need to be to receive His blessings. The trials and tribulations that tarnish our lives come not to defeat, but only that God may be lifted. God is lifted up and glorified when we humble ourselves to Him and ask for His forgiveness and His help. We can withstand anything life throws our way as long as we are holding on to the anchor. The anchor can keep us steadfast and immovable. God is ready, willing, and able to bless us, but He needs to know that we will handle the blessing with care. He needs to know that we will not brag or boast with a puffed up chest as if we are responsible for our own blessings. He wants to get the glory, and He should get the glory because it was He who provided the blessings and not ourselves.

And God is able to make all grace abound toward you; that ye, always having all sufficiency in all things, may abound to every good work: 9 (As it is written, He hath dispersed abroad; he hath given to the poor: his righteousness remaineth for ever. 10 Now he that ministereth seed to the sower both minister bread for your food, and multiply your seed sown, and increase the fruits of your righteousness;) 11 Being enriched in every thing to all bountifulness, which causeth through us thanksgiving to God.
2 Corinthians 9:8-11

It's all about the choices we make and the steps we take to make the most of our blessings. Begin and end every situation with prayer, and God will direct your path. God hears our every prayer, and He stands ready to answer your call. The best thing about calling on the name of the Lord is you will never face unavailability. We may not always make ourselves available to God, but He is still available to each of us. The more we lean and depend on Him, the more we will lean on Him. We tend to follow others in life when they are making a difference, but this may not be the route God wants us to take. It is the comfort we feel when following God which lets us know we are on the right path. Following others has no promises, following God has unlimited guarantees for all. Don't be your own blessing blocker by living in the past. Unlock the blessings God has for you by following His lead from Earth to Glory. Let nothing turn you around once you decide to follow Jesus, not your past, not your future, not your circumstances, not your wavering faith, nor your un-beliefs. You should only remember the things of the past to encourage yourself or to encourage others. Your history should be a path which leads you to a brighter future. God's lamp lights your way. It should be used as a gauge to measure how far God has brought you and a compass to focus on where He is taking you. If it hadn't been for the Lord on my side, I don't know where I would be today. Take a selfie of your life, and count up the blessings you capture, develop them one by one. Put praise on each of the blessings to see what God has done.

Blessed is the man that trusteth in the Lord, and whose hope the Lord is.
Jeremiah 17:7

35 I have shewed you all things, how that so labouring ye ought to support the weak, and to remember the words of the Lord Jesus, how he said, It is more blessed to give than to receive."
Acts 20: 35

> Lord, thank You for blessing me even when I didn't deserve it. Thank You for giving me the desire to want to be a blessing to others. Help me to always be cheerful as You bless me. I thank you for blessing me more than I could ever live to deserve. May the blessing bestowed upon me be paid forwardly to meet the needs of others. Keep me balanced in Your word and Your works. Keep me stable in the space you provide for me. It is with great thanksgiving that I render this pray unto you. Amen.

MY CLAIM IS NOT TO FAME

Chapter Twelve

Life has a way of inflating our pride and puffing up our egos, giving us a false sense of "we've arrived." We live life competing for things that are of little to no value at all. Spending time competing for status or mundane objects is a waste of time if it's only for self-gain. When we compete, it should be for the betterment of people and not ourselves. God did not create us to be an island. He created us to work, strive for the improvement of people, and to be all-inclusive. We receive more grace from God than we can fathom when we work, displaying love and acceptance of all. Our Father in Heaven is rich, and when we became His children, we inherited His glorious riches. There is no more abundant or more famous life; you will ever be able to live than a life with Jesus. This is all the fame I will ever need. Oh, how I long to be like Him and to please Him in all I do, without Him, nothing in life has any actual value. There are times in life where money and other mundane items go unclaimed, they hold no value compared to the Savior we claim.

19 Lay not up for yourselves treasures upon earth, where moth and rust corrupt, and where thieves break through and steal: 20 But lay up for yourselves treasures in Heaven, where neither moth nor rust corrupt, and where thieves do not break through nor steal: 21 For where you treasure is, there will your heart be also.

Matthew 6: 19- 21

But seek ye first the kingdom of God and his righteousness, and all these things shall be added unto you.
Matthew 6: 33-

3 Blessed are the poor in spirit: for theirs is the kingdom of Heaven. 4 Blessed are they that mourn: for they shall be comforted. 5 Blessed are the meek: for they shall inherit the earth. 6 Blessed are they which do hunger and thirst after righteousness: for they shall be filled. 7 Blessed are the merciful: for they shall obtain mercy. 8 Blessed are the pure in heart: for they shall see God. 9 Blessed are the peacemakers: for they shall be called the children of God. 10 Blessed are they which are persecuted for righteousness' sake: for theirs is the kingdom of Heaven.
Matthew 5: 3-10

Lord, thank You for leaving the Bible as a blueprint for me to build a life with You. Thank You for leaving no doubt or questions about what it means to be a child of God. I pray that You will continue to work with me and through me to keep me on track. I know that you are not finished with me yet, but I want to be accessible to you and for You. Keep me meditating on Your word and using your name to encourage others as I travel on this journey. Use me as you see fit, and I will give you all the honor, glory, and praise that only You deserve. This and all blessings I ask in the mighty name of Jesus Christ. Amen.

A Stormy Epiphany

UNEQUIVOCALLY POWERFUL

Chapter Thirteen

The day I made up my mind to let go and let God was the best day of my life. I started out at an early age living with the fear of coming to God because I didn't want to disappoint God. I feared God greatly in a respectful way, and I thought I needed to fix me before coming to Him. Don't waste your time, I wasted mine! It's not your job to fix you, just as it wasn't my job to fix me. God is God all by Himself, and He doesn't need help fixing us up. There is no doubt about the power of God and His ability to make right all our wrongs. He only needs you and me to come to Him just as we are and acknowledge He is Lord, confess our sins, and leave the rest up to Him. He takes delight in knowing we recognize our weaknesses and need his strength to make it. The Bible tells us in **2 Corinthians 12:9-11**, *"My grace is sufficient for you, my strength is made perfect in weakness."* I look to the Lord, knowing He will provide me with strength for the task. I will fall in love with Jesus over and over again, He knows my heart.

God loved us before we even learned how to love our selves. He leads by example; He first loved us and showed us what it truly means to love. He has given us a guide, and He does not conceal the path which leads from earth to glory. Instead, he makes the path of righteousness accessible and viewable for all to see and make a choice to travel. He is the light of the world, and with Him, the darkness of life will be evaded forever.

Then spake Jesus again unto them, saying, I am the light of the world: he who followeth me shall not walk in darkness, but shall have the light of life.

John 8:12

Have you ever felt as if no one had the time of day for you? Well, God is not like that, He's available twenty-four hours a day, seven days a week. We must make ourselves available to Him. He doesn't require us to jump through hoops to reach Him like individuals sometimes do. He stands ready, willing, and able to get us through times of despair, sorrow, troubles, depression, and disappointments. He is also the God who rejoices with us in every milestone, victory, accomplishment, and salvation.

We spend a lifetime taking chances on everything presented to us. Why is it so complicated to make the decision to take a chance on Jesus? He believes in us enough to give us a chance after chance to get right with Him. He knows all the things that will happen before they happen. Our job is to trust Him with all our hearts. The immensity of His love is far beyond anything we could ever imagine. We may never comprehend why He loves us so much, but we should spend eternity singing His praises because He does. The power our Father possesses is above all power. What manner of man is this that even the winds obey and cease to blow when He speaks?

Thine, O Lord is the greatness, and the power, and the glory, and the victory, and the majesty: for all that is in the Heaven and in the earth is thine; thine is the kingdom, O Lord, and thou art exalted as head above all.
1 Chronicles: 29:11

> Lord, thank You for loving me and giving me a chance after chance to get right with you. Please keep my heart and mind tuned into Your purpose and plan for my life. Teach me to listen for your voice and to be obedient to your words. Thank You for loving me when I didn't know how to love myself. I pray that You will be pleased with my praises unto You. In Jesus' name, I pray. Amen.

PHENOMENAL PRAISE
Chapter Fourteen

When we take the time to think about God and all He does for the good of those who love Him, it is nothing less than remarkable. He starts out by giving us a compass (the Bible) to navigate to the path which leads us to a life of abundance. The more we study His word and follow the plan and purpose He has for us, the more we find ourselves wanting to follow Him. When we are consistent with our prayers to God, asking for guidance, He will always deliver us to where we need to be to accomplish His plan for our lives. No one knows better than God, where we are supposed to be, and no one can deliver us as He can. He can and will deliver us from whatever we need to be delivered from. If it's a pain, He can do it, if it's brokenness, He can do it; if it's bondage, He can do it; if it's doubt, He can do it; if it's fear, He can do it. Yes, He remains faithful in all He promises. What will it take for us to stay loyal to our God? The more you give to God, the more He gives to you and the more you want to give to Him.

The spirit of God primes our pump for giving, but that spirit is sometimes out of order. These are the times when we must immerse in the wells of our faith and ask God to supply us with a fresh anointing of His Holy Spirit. This will ignite the desire to give God a portion of what He has given to us. God has given us the ultimate gift that keeps on giving. By sending His only begotten son to die for our sins is proof positive of the love given us.

I'm so glad God loves us because of who He is and not because of who we are. What a mighty God we serve!! His praises shall never cease from within me. I will praise God with all my heart and everything within me.

I have landed in some comfortable places in my life and some cramped spaces. No matter where I find myself dealing with the living, God is there.

7 Whither shall I go from thy spirit? or whither shall I flee from thy presence? 8 If I ascend up into Heaven, thou art there: if I make my bed in hell, behold, thou art there. 9 If I take the wings of the morning, and dwell in the uttermost parts of the sea; 10 Even there shall thy hand lead me, and thy right hand shall hold me.
Psalm 139: 7-10

I no longer have to sit back and wonder how I will make it from one experience to another because I know my God will meet every single need. I have lived long enough to realize everything I've experienced in life was necessary for my spiritual growth. The development of a spiritual being takes a certain amount of time, task, commitment, and perseverance. Let go and let God work in you and through you to ignite the light He desires to see, illuminate from within you. We are to immerse ourselves in the word of God's teachings to complete our Heavenly Father's earthly task as he would desire. The praises we give unto God should be full of energy and joy. The joy God allows to penetrate our hearts when we don't deserve it is merely incredible. Our praises sent up to Him should be much more incredible. The more praises we send-up, the more blessings He sends down. I'm not telling you what I've heard, I'm telling you what I'm living!

In our everyday lives, most of us don't realize God is busy at work running interference on dangers that lie ahead in our paths.

We are to praise Him in advance for whenever and however He may decide to bless us. We all worship God in different ways; the most important thing is that you get your praise on. I may praise God through my silent tears, shaking my head and the patting of my foot and you may glorify Him by calling out to Him; there is no little praise or big praise, the only real praise is the true praise that comes from the heart.

Lord, thank You for thinking enough of us to leave with us a comforter called the Holy Spirit. Thank You for loving us so much that You promise never to leave us alone. Please help us to always remember to give You and only You the praise that You are so worthy of. Let us praise You so that the rocks will not cry out for us. Thank You for delivering us from so many places, so many times. Help us to adopt the agape kind of love that You shower us with every day. In Jesus' name, we pray. Amen.

RIDING THE WAVES

Chapter Fifteen

The roller coaster rides of life can often leave us a little shaken, not knowing which way to turn. The bumps and bruises we are left with could dampen our spirits if we are not careful. The fact you give your life to God and are resting in His love does not exempt you from trials and tribulations. This submission provides you comfort in knowing you will never be left to ride out the storms alone. I have spent countless days and nights grumbling over bumps and bruises I had no control over. It took lots of time and effort in prayer to finally gain an appreciation for my bumps and bruises, which led me to unimaginable healings for my spirit, soul, and body. It's these uncomfortable events that teach us to seek God first in everything we do before we decide to do it. It's these band aid bruises that act as reminders of how grateful I am to God for picking me up every time I fell. The imperfections are a daily reminder of how much I need God every second of the day. We must cultivate an attitude of gratitude. The glory belongs to God every time He turns a situation around in our favor. No matter which way the winds of life blow you, God will be right there to catch you, He's got it like that. He knows all we will experience in life. He is a good Father, He works in your life, and my life to prepare us for what is to come.

28 Come unto me, all ye that labour and are heavy laden, and I will give you rest. 29 Take my yoke upon you, and learn of me; for I am meek and lowly in heart: and ye shall find rest unto your souls. 30 For my yoke is easy, and my burden is light. **Matthew: 11:28-30**

It behooves us to stay in tune with God and stay near to Him. He never leaves us, so if you think you've discovered He is not near, you obviously have left Him. This is the time when you will need to re-direct your course.

The rough waves we experience through the storms of our lives are preparing us for the tsunami's that are to come. God is so kind and so loving. He only allows what He knows we can handle and no more. He starts out by allowing the thunderstorms before He will allow the tsunamis to bounce in our lives. We need to know our own character on how we respond to thunderstorms first, then see God work in our lives to prepare us for more devastating storms. The more we face, the stronger we become, but our strength is not build on one experience. The bigger the storms, the greater the faith in the aftermath.

> *5 But if any of you lacks wisdom, let him ask of God, who gives to all generously and without reproach, and it will be given to him. 6 But he must ask in faith without any doubting, for the one who doubts is like the surf of the sea, driven and tossed by the wind*
> **James 1:5-6**

God shows us in all He does, we are precious in His sight. We are all sinners saved by God's amazing grace. He is so forgiving as he forgets the sin, but never the sinner. Whenever there was trouble in my way, God sent His helpers Grace and Mercy to renew my strength until the problem was removed. When my friends were few, and I couldn't see my way, a voice would whisper sweet peace to me. When I thought I was lost and couldn't find my way, all I did was cry out precious Lord take my hand. Jesus is real to me, and He has opened so many doors for me, and I'm sure He has done the same for you. All we have to do is hold onto God's unchanging hand and keep the faith of a mustard seed and everything will be alright. Know for sure, God provides us with wings of love to ride the waves until our storms pass over. Those wings are His words and promises found in the Bible. I love the song entitled *Ride out the Storm*. I absolutely love hymns. I get lost in the words of the old-time hymns of the church especially when I require encouragement. Some of my favorites are *Pass Me Not O Gentle Savior, Blessed Assurance, Yes, God is Real, My Hope is Built, What a Friend We Have in Jesus,* and last but not least *Amazing Grace.* These songs speak peace to my soul. The words of these songs lighten any dark place in life and give hope to the hopeless. I know beyond a shadow of a doubt I would never have made it without God.

Lord, thank You for carrying me through the storms. Thank You for instilling hope and expectation within me. I pray that all I do and all I ever hope to be will be found in Your loving and forgiving spirit. Please help me to hold someone else's hand while they are riding out their storm. Help me to be the beacon of hope that they need to see their way. These and all the blessings I ask in Your precious name. Amen.

A Stormy Epiphany

CHOOSING THE HIGH ROAD

Chapter Sixteen

As we live, experience, and grow through the weeds of life, we discover we're on spiritual life support. We go through trials and tribulations, setbacks, and setups only to find ourselves on the lane of despair. Therefore, it is vitally important to be wrapped up and tied up in the word of God. Life will beat you down, but the truths of God's Holy Word will pick you up and sustain you for the long haul. We must not be caught unprepared to stand against the wiles of the devil when he comes to create havoc on our lives. It's like taking a test, your results are as good as your preparation, as my grandson quickly reminded me. The one who is equipped with the full armor of God will be able to stand. It is the same way with our faith, the more we study, meditate, digest, and apply the word to our lives, the stronger our faith will become. Doubt creeps into our minds to challenge everything we believe, but the word that is embedded in our hearts and paints our souls will take precedence over the uncertainty our mind entertains. Just pray without ceasing.

8 Finally brothers, whatever is pure, whatever is noble, whatever is right, whatever is pure whatever is lovely, whatever is admirable- if anything is excellent or praiseworthy – think about such things. 9 Whatever you have learned or received or heard from me or seen in me put it into practice. And the God of peace will be with you.
Philippians: 4:8-9

The mind must stay engaged with things which are excellent and pleasing to God so our actions will emulate what His word says. We must make it a determination to protect our minds with positive, productive thoughts. Afterall, what goes in the mind will definitely come out, and when it does, we want no regrets. We should not only practice what we preach but more importantly, we must practice what God teaches. We can hear a sermon any day, and sometimes we forget it before we leave it, but the sermon we live will be the one remembered the most when it's all said and done. How would you like to be remembered?

The more we meditate on the word of God and practice being obedient to what the word says, the more we will become convicted by the name. At some point, we have the time of our lives and think life couldn't get any better. Well, I come to tell you that unless you have met the Savior of the world, you haven't begun to live yet. Don't get me wrong, I once thought I was living the life to be lived as well, only to find out that I was sadly mistaken. The best party you could ever experience is a Holy Ghost party. The party of your life begins when you get to know the Savior and to know the Man is to love Him. People often ask me why I have a smile on my face? I tell them, it's because of the smile on my heart that God has permanently placed there because of His love and forgiveness to me. It's because he continues to send the twins grace and mercy to rescue me. He bestows so much upon me, and undeserving vessel such as myself.

The nature of mankind is to please those whom we love, but the humanity of man makes it difficult to please God as we should. It must be intentionally a work in progress. The more we work at it, the more we will want to work at it. God knows our struggles. He knows we will never reach perfection because He is the only perfect one. One thing we must train our minds, hearts, and souls to believe is that we must choose the side of righteousness to follow Christ. It's not easy because we must work with our imperfections and the imperfections of others, but we have a willing helper; all we have to do is ask. Starting now, put your soul on notice, tell your soul, "I refuse to allow you to be lost." Take control of your soul's salvation and be removed from life support, you will survive.

> *I beseech you therefore, brethren, by the mercies of God, that ye present your bodies a living sacrifice, holy, acceptable unto God, which is your reasonable service. 2 And be not conformed to this world: but be ye transformed by the renewing of your mind, that ye may prove what is that good, and acceptable, and perfect, will of God..* **Romans: 12:1-2**

You will indeed survive the wiles of the devil because you have the protection of the Almighty; case closed. I am blessed beyond measure, not because I am kind, but because God is so good and because His love for me is everlasting. This that I write is not of me, it is of my Heavenly Father and the love He demonstrates for me and my love for Him. It is of God, from God, about God and how He has made a believer out of me. It is to tell you that He can and will bless you beyond anything you can imagine, just as He has me. It is to express to you about how He first loved us, even knowing how imperfect we were. It's about taking this opportunity to share God's goodness with others who otherwise may not know. Though words are inadequate to describe His love for us, I use what I have to make an attempt. To express His love for us through the many acts of undeserving kindness extended to each of us. I often think of my sisters and brothers in laws adopting the name given to me by my husband from the moment they met me. To this day, they refer to me by no other name than "Debbie Luv." With my extended family, there was a shared love which came so naturally. This kind of love is what our Heavenly Father desires we share with our family of believers.

The love that my kids and I receive from our extended family is one that I cherish and will never take for granted. You must be able to give love to receive love. Only God could have placed me in a family that would love my kids and me unconditionally and give us such a sense of belonging. I call them Sisters-n-LOVE and Brothers-n-LOVE because while the law established us as sisters and brothers, it's the love that keeps us as sisters and brothers. The love that nurtures you while growing up will not depart from you. I thank God for my loving mother, daddy, and grandmother, who did their very best to teach my siblings and me how to love God, ourselves, and each other. This is the kind of love God desires us to have for one another. We, the family of believers must love one another unconditionally as God loves us. We must live by example. Anyone can say, "I love you," but only those who know the love of God can display love as it is intended to be.

Father almighty, it is my determination to let nothing turn me away from Your love. Thank You for giving me the right to the tree of life. It is my desire to love, serve, obey, and trust You with everything within me. Because You live, I know that I, too, can live and be abundantly blessed in your name. Help me serve You in spirit and in truth. Let everything that I do for You be real. Help me to love as You love. Keep me in your word and keep my thoughts in a safe place. In Jesus' name, I pray. Amen.

CLINGING TO THE ROCK
Chapter Seventeen

As breathing, developing, and articulate beings, we have to utilize each day given to us to grow closer to the Rock and to travel the high road. Our foundation and salvation are found in Jesus Christ. **Psalms 62**:2 (AMP) tells us, *"He alone is my rock and my salvation, my defense and my strong tower; I will not be shaken or disheartened."*

Our goal must be to gain progress in the Army for the Lord. As long as we keep moving forward and looking toward the things before us, we should not lose focus. A little progress is better than no progress at all. The more we work in the Army of the Lord, the more we work toward bringing the things of God to the masses. We know the only sure thing in life is Christ. He is the same yesterday, today, and forever. Our benefit is to position ourselves on the foundation of the solid rock. I genuinely believe that things in our lives transpire for a reason. One reason is purpose-driven, and another is for God to get the glory He deserves.

Anything God allows, He has a purpose for it. In our purposeful line of events, He teaches us how to respond to unfavorable circumstances. We are taught through the Scripture that *in all things, give thanks*, no matter how dim things may appear. This shows us to trust our Heavenly Father for all things. On the other hand, we initiate purposeless events that lead to something that ends up wasting precious time, not to mention the cost we pay for these lifeless events. I have made a lot of mistakes, but it was not a mistake to take the time to ponder the words of wisdom vehemently ringing in my ears through my mother and grandmother. It was no mistake when I listened to fatherly advice from my daddy, though I thought I knew how to plan my future. It was no mistake when God allowed the words of wisdom to penetrate the deepest crevices of my heart. It was not a mistake that God opened my spiritual eyes to see my unspiritual acts. It was no mistake that God saw fit to give me a story to share. The snippets of advice my mother and grandmother gave on how God is always with me picked me up every time I fell. These wise sayings taught me to forget my circumstances and remember my God. Yes, MY GOD; for their God has become MY GOD. The never-ceasing prayers of the faithful kept me believing and expecting my God to show up and show out.

I needed direction then, Lord knows I need even more guidance to follow God. The closer one gets to God, the harder one fights to keep the devil at bay. He has no need to fight for those who are self-serving or serving anyone other than God. The enemy works to change your direction. You see, it didn't require many courses when I wasn't following anyone or wasn't going anywhere. I just did my own thing and ended up where I ended up. Now, I have a desire to get it, because I am following the right leader, the one who is above all, so yes, I need lots of direction. God is waiting and willing to lead us from Earth to glory; we must make the decision to take Him at His word. We must make a choice to follow Him.

> *But seek ye first the kingdom of God and his righteousness, and all these things shall be added unto you.* **Matthew 6:33**

God gives us a compass for a reason. He doesn't want our lives to be lost without a cause. He has given us what we need to find our way to the Savior and life everlasting. We must instill a sense of priority into our daily communion with our Heavenly Father. We should seek out that which is righteous and Holy with a sense of intentionality.

> *5 And beside this, giving all diligence, add to your faith virtue; and to virtue knowledge; 6 And to knowledge temperance; and to temperance patience; and to patience godliness; 7 And to godliness brotherly kindness; and to brotherly kindness charity. 8 For if these things be in you, and abound, they make you that ye shall neither be barren nor unfruitful in the knowledge of our Lord Jesus Christ. 9 But he that lacketh these things is blind, and cannot see afar off, and hath forgotten that he was purged from his old sins.*
>
> *10 Wherefore the rather, brethren, give diligence to make your calling and election sure: for if ye do these things, ye shall never fall: 11 For so an entrance shall be ministered unto you abundantly into the everlasting kingdom of our Lord and Saviour Jesus Christ.*
>
> **2 Peter: 1:5-11**

Father, thank You for giving me everything I need to get to know You better. Thank You for giving me what I need to make my way to You. Thank you for mapping out the path that leads to a life of safety in your arms. I praise You and honor Your most righteous name. Please give me the strength to continue to hold onto the solid rock, for You are my rock and my salvation. Help me to pull someone up who has fallen. In Jesus' name, I pray. Amen.

IT'S A LOVE THING

Chapter Eighteen

It is a comfort knowing no matter what we are faced with, once the decision is made to cling to the Solid Rock, we needn't be afraid. We make the decisions to do things we shouldn't or should do, But God is ever present to help us in times of need. He is dependable to lean on. The times when we are farthest from God is the time His never-failing love reaches us. His love reaches out to get us back to the place where we need to be. There isn't a place we can go to escape God's presence, no matter how hard we try. God is always everywhere, and nothing can separate us from His love.

> *8 If I go up to the Heavens, you are there. 9 If I rise on the wings of the dawn, If I settle on the far side of the sea, 10 even there your hand will guide me, your right hand will hold me fast. 11 If I say, "Surely the darkness will hide me and the light become night around me," 12 even the darkness will not be dark to you; the night will shine like the day, for darkness is as light to you. 13 For you created my inmost being, you knit me together in my mother's womb. 14 I praise you because I am wonderfully made; your works are beautiful; I know that full well.*
>
> **Psalm 139:8-13**

God deserves our thanksgiving whether we feel like it or not. He is constantly showering us with His unconditional love, mercy, and grace. When you find yourself in the lowest of valleys with your faith, God's love will greet you there. When you are on *"Disappointment Drive"* with your finances, God will show up there and make a way because HE IS THE WAY! When you're on the highest peak of the mountaintop with your peace, God is there. There will arise difficult situations that will wear you down, but God's love will build you up, help you to stand, and lead you on your way.

Though I speak with the tongues of men and of angels, and have not charity, I am become as sounding brass, or a tinkling cymbal. 2 And though I have the gift of prophecy, and understand all mysteries, and all knowledge; and though I have all faith, so that I could remove mountains, and have not charity, I am nothing. 3 And though I bestow all my goods to feed the poor, and though I give my body to be burned, and have not charity, it profiteth me nothing. 4 Charity suffereth long, and is kind; charity envieth not; charity vaunteth not itself, is not puffed up, 5 Doth not behave itself unseemly, seeketh not her own, is not easily provoked, thinketh no evil; 6 Rejoiceth not in iniquity, but rejoiceth in the truth; 7 Beareth all things, believeth all things, hopeth all things, endureth all things.8 Charity never faileth: but whether there be prophecies, they shall fail; whether there be tongues, they shall cease; whether there be knowledge, it shall vanish away.
1 Corinthians 13: 1-8

We must learn to put our faith and hope in things that will stand the test of time. It is much easier said than done, but the more we demonstrate the love of Jesus Christ in our daily lives, the stronger we will become in the faith and hope of our Father. We can all take part in playing a role in showing a little more love. Everyone wants to receive love, so why not start out by giving some love? Just as a newborn baby grows and feels the love of a mother or father, we as adults can be comforted when we receive this kind of love and comfort from our Heavenly Father.

God gives each of us different gifts, but the gift of love is given to all. Demonstrating respect for others doesn't come easy for everyone, some people will have to work harder than others to reach the point of showing love. Some people make it difficult when we attempt to show appreciation to them, but that's where the love of God within you will show up and cause you to love them anyway. Be patient with others as they grow to get to where you are, God is certainly patient with us. The love you show may draw someone closer to Christ, or the appreciation you refuse to show may push them further away. It's all about others feeling the love of Christ at work in you from the inside out. This is called AGAPE. No credit of mine, nor yours, it's all about the love of Christ and His goodness. We must learn to love despite our flaws. It's not enough to love through the natural instincts like eros (romantic love) or phileos (friendship or sibling love), or even storge (parental love), but we should ask God to do the supernatural AGAPE love. The AGAPE love is the God-kind of love. It encompasses all the kinds of love and it will then be easy to love those who we know have despitefully used and abused us. This magnitude of love can come only from a Holy power of an awesome God.

You don't have real love if you're only capable of loving those whom you know love you. Remember to show love in all you do. The moment you fail to show love could be the moment you lose the person who was almost persuaded.

Heavenly Father, I thank You for uniquely loving me. You show so much love for me even when I don't deserve it. You are love, and everything about you symbolizes Your great love for us. Help us to give meaning to the love that we show others as you show unto us. Please don't let our lack of love remove us from your presence. Help us to reach others as we continue this journey in life. Don't let our living be in vain. Let our lights so shine that others are led to unite with you. This is your servant's prayer. Amen

INDELIBLE TRANSFORMATION

Chapter Nineteen

In taking inventory of our lives to make better choices, we may start out looking and working in all the wrong places, but the moment we look to Jesus for His guidance and protection, we will see transformation taking place. With this kind of transformation, no one is capable of touching it once God stamps His seal of approval on it. When God changes us, nothing compares to the change we experience.

God's salvation is free to all because Jesus paid the price; it is not something that pops up on you like an unexpected guest. The door stands open, and the invitation is extended. The choice is yours to make. The acceptance of the invitation is the beginning of your transformation. Everything is new, and all old things pass away. When I look back over my life, I can only thank God for all the things He made fresh in my life. The chance to receive a brand-new set of mercies every day is nothing short of a miracle. Only God can perform miraculous acts of love and kindness extended to us each day.

Thinking over things that happened in our lives, and if we took the time to dissect the innermost feelings about how things played out, we would confess that we are better than blessed. The number of self-inflicted heartaches we endure are far more than we care to remember, and yet God still gives us mercy. Although we make bad choices that reap havoc on our lives and the lives of others, God in His awesomeness always gives us another chance. It is up to us to engage opportunities to see our transformations through. No one knows when their chance will be the last one. We are wise to take each chance at love to love unconditionally, take each opportunity to forgive, and forgive without exceptions. We are wise to make the choice to give, making sure not to give out of necessity. We are even more careful to take the chance to serve with humility and gratitude, not to serve out of selfish expectations.

God is ready, willing, and able to replenish our resources when they become depleted. These are the times we must not yield to temptation, rather resist the desire to operate on our own resources. The more we depend on God for His love, guidance, protection, and His strength, the more we will rely on Him for His love, guidance, protection, and strength. We grow closer and more intimate with God through the difficulties we endure. God's glory, power, and grace shines brighter for all to see in our darkest hours.

When we are left in awe as a result of our *"made a way out of no way"* experiences, featuring the Almighty God, we are left transformed like none other. There are no doubts, no questions, no misinterpretations, or no miscommunications about who has all power in his hands. We are on track when we pray, trust, and follow the Lord's guidance for our lives. He is all we need to be fully equipped to have victory every time in any war in our lives and the lives of our kindred.

Lie not one to another, seeing that ye have put off the old man with his deeds; And have put on the new man, which is renewed in knowledge after the image of him that created him:
Colossians 3:9-10

God's mercy is the light guiding us when we are lost in darkness with no hope in sight. He guides us back to the throne of grace when we go astray. It may be a dark cloud over your health, family matters, or your job. In times like these, God will give you a story (testimony) to share with others who may feel the same hopelessness. Take advantage of what God is doing in your life and receive the lesson intended for you. You will learn to pull the good from a not-so-good situation and hold on to it as a lesson learned. You will learn to sift out the bad; sharing those stories with others to show how God turned things around in your life and give them hope for their own situation.

Lord give us a fresh anointing of Your Holy Spirit. Thank You for teaching us that there's good in every situation. Thank You for giving us hope in a dying world. Thank You for keeping my mind staying on You and Your amazing grace. Teach me how to protect each chance that You give me and share with others to bring You glory. Let not our minds be led astray, but keep our minds, hearts, and souls in tune with Your will for our lives. Thank You for Your loving-kindness. In Jesus' name, I pray. Amen.

SAVORING THE SEASON

Chapter Twenty

As we try to plan our lives the way we feel they should play out, we will soon find out that if our plans are not in line with God's plans, they will never come to fruition. I have learned the hard way through trial and error, no matter how well thought out my plans are, it's not enough if God is not the orchestrator. As a young adult, I went about my business making plans for the family life I thought was at hand, but the plans were never brought to God in prayer. A great example of how God's plans are not our plans. I failed miserably, but God never failed me, He never stopped loving me. It hit me like a ton of bricks when I realized I only needed to go to God in prayer and ask for his guidance and for His will to be done. After being transformed by the Holy Spirit, it became easy to go to God in prayer to ask His will in every situation of my life. I wasn't perfect then, and I'm far from perfect now, but I trust and lean on the One Who Is, and the One who transforms. God can give you what you need for elevation, not for selfishness, but elevation for service.

Seek God in all your ways, and when you seek Him, you must savor those moments in the meditation of His words.

We stand to profit the most from spending quiet time with God. I've found when I focus entirely on God and close off other corners of the world, I receive the greatest blessings. The blessings of forgiveness, peace, direction, and the help of security, are all benefits of an intimate relationship with God. The things God reveals may knock you off your feet, just be ready to embrace whatever He sends your way. When we ask God to keep us, He will hold us closer than close. He won't let go and we're close because we want to be. Without God's guidance and protection, we are lost without a hope. In God, we find a sense of belonging, purpose, worth, and direction. Bask in the season of your life which God is working on at this moment. Don't lose out on your blessings because you have moved on ahead of Him to a next season.

1 I waited patiently for the Lord; and he inclined unto me, and heard my cry. 2 He brought me up also out of an horrible pit, out of the miry clay, and set my feet upon a rock, and established my goings. 3 And he hath put a new song in my mouth, even praise unto our God: many shall see it, and fear, and shall trust in the Lord. 4 Blessed is that man that maketh the Lord his trust, and respecteth not the proud, nor such as turn aside to lies.

Psalm 40:1-4

Lord, thank You for the patience You extend to me when I'm doing everything except what You have called me to do. Keep me in Your care and help me to show patience to others. Lord, don't let me move to hastily and forget to sing praises unto You. Instill within me a spirit of gratitude for all the little things you give to me. Bless me and help me to always savor the season of praise. Help me to always encourage and bless others. This is your servant's prayer. Amen

THE GOSSIPING TRUTH
Chapter Twenty-one

Some of the most motivating experiences will come from conversations with a child. Children are among one the most honest groups of people you will ever approach. Unless taught otherwise, children speak of what they know to be the truth, as far as their understanding of what they see. If you ever need an honest opinion on anything, ask a child. The Bible speaks about how a child shall lead, and there are some lessons we can learn from our kids. Children's natural personalities are like the Bible; full of truths until something or someone distorts the truth to make it say what they want it to say.

In my opinion, the Bible is not an easy read, but the more it's read, the more discernment will reveal the understanding of His truths. There are lots of things we run to tell, but none can hold a candle to the truth of God's word. There are no shortages in carriers of bad news. Let us be intentional about being suitable news carriers. There are folk who are excited to get the good news out about the goodness of the Lord. I can remember riding in my car one afternoon with my five year old baby girl. She was a very talkative and extremely curious little one. She tried to get my attention, but because I was so preoccupied with life, it took me a moment before I realized she called out to me. When I finally answered, she said, "Mommy, now I can't remember what I had to tell you because you weren't paying attention." I replied, "Sweetie, it's ok," and she responded, "But mom, I don't know if it was important or not." After a silent chuckle, I responded by saying, "Sweetie, if it was necessary, it will come back to you." I often think about that day and ask myself, "Are you listening when God talks? Are you paying attention when He speaks and moves in your life"? Everything God has to say is of the utmost importance. We should take a timeout sometimes and ask ourselves the question if we are too busy with life to hear from God? My baby girl, Kanesha, reminded me that day, that we can be so caught up with life that it passes us by. I don't want the master to pass me by, I want Him to hear my humble cry.

23 But the hour cometh, and now is, when the true worshippers shall worship the Father in spirit and in truth: for the Father seeketh such to worship him.

24 God is a Spirit: and they that worship him must worship him in spirit and in truth.

John 4: 23-24

Dear children, let us not love with words or tongue but with actions and in truth. (19) This then is how we know we belong to the fact and how we set our hearts at rest in his presence.

***1* John 3:18-19**

Jesus answered, I am the way and the truth and the life. No one comes to the Father except through me. (7) If you really knew me, you would know my Father as well. From now on, you do know him and have seen him.

John 14: 6-7

But when he, the spirit of truth, comes, he will guide you into all truth. He will not speak on his own; he will speak what he hears, and he will tell you what is yet to come.   **John 16: 13**

Yes, God's word is full of truths we can gossip about throughout the land until eternity. This is the kind of gossip that we all must be deliberate about spreading. Let us all gossip about the truth of the good news that our Savior lives.

Father God, thank You for making Your truths available for me. Thank You for blessing me to a measure beyond my imagination. Father, keep me leaning on and living on your divine truths. Don't let me get it twisted or try to re-write the script, help me to delve into your text, and gain discernment from your Holy words. Teach me to spread the good news of Your love to those that I come into contact with. In Jesus' name, I pray. Amen.

WORKING THE MESSAGE

Chapter Twenty-two

It's not always easy to speak about spirituality and salvation in specific settings. We want to share the good news concerning hope for all with Jesus Christ, but we are reluctant to do so because we fear rejection. I accepted that I may be dismissed or simply turned away when speaking about the life that words can only attempt to describe. The fear I once carried I no longer bear, because of how great God has been and continues to be. Period.

In 2nd Timothy, 1st chapter 7th verse, the Bible tells us *"For God hath not given us the spirit of fear; but of power, and of love and of a sound mind."*

I remind myself daily, I can no longer allow fear to hinder me from doing what God called me to do. The Lord and I partner to work where He has designated for me; the space which is tailored just for me. I will spend the rest of my days occupying that space with my name on it. I practice working outside the box to get myself out of my comfort zone. The comfort zone limits you to only what you can do within your natural powers. The outer area will force you to rely on supernatural powers that come from God. The message of the "GOOD NEWS" must be heard from you and me. We can't afford for the word to get trapped within the walls of the church and stay there. The message must go beyond the walls. It is easy for someone to give or get a message in the church, but how easy is it to get a piece of news on the street? This is where you and I come in; taking every opportunity to tell everyone about our God. We must be willing to testify where God has brought us from, how He continues to bless us over and over, how He never leaves us or forsake us, how He makes way for us when we can't see our way, and how he loves us despite our shortcomings. We must be bold enough to share those shortcomings while revealing the power of God. This lifts Him up.

We were not all designed to work the same spaces, that's why we are in different places so the message will be disseminated from throughout; place to place. We must incorporate innovative methods of communication to reach the masses. We fully understand not everyone will be willing to listen to our testimonies, but don't give up. There is more than one way to deliver a message. This prompts us to get our creative juices flowing for indirect conversations on the grace of God. I can remember time and time again asking the question, "God, why am I in this place?" As I matured in the faith and learned how to talk and listen to God, I now say "God, I know you have me in this place for a reason and I'm going to pray until something happens."

My employer has an annual training titled "Growing Better Together" to assist colleagues in developing practical communications skills, message delivery methods, and recognizing and accepting acts of accountability. This training session also strives to build acceptance and understanding of diversity and inclusion. This creates a more positive, productive, and cohesive work environment. Just as my employer recognizes the strength in unity and agrees, everyone has something to offer. God expects us to work and grow together to create a more positive and loving world. He also knows when we make it a priority to grow closer to Him, it will make it easier to grow closer to others and be more accepting of others. We have more to gain by following company policies and procedures, just as we have more to gain following God's commandments. We may shed some blood, sweat, and tears throughout the process, but after all, no pain, no gain.

In past years when asked to facilitate training sessions at work, I became very nervous. My first thought would be to decline. Although I believe strongly in the efforts made to strive for diversity and inclusiveness, I was still reluctant to take on the task. Now, I see this as part of God's plan for me stepping out of the box and taking advantage of the platform I've been given. Although I am still quite nervous initially, I embrace the challenge and thank God for entrusting me with the opportunity. The facilitating may be job-related, but the facilitator in me is God originated. This is one of those outer box examples God has blessed me with to work His message through me. God can deliver a message through whomever He chooses, and the message can be verbal or nonverbal. He can go beyond the original message and pull out the word within the message.

When I think back, I can remember working on my son and daughter to be effective, proficient public speakers starting at an early age. I wanted to help them avoid growing up with the fear I had. I knew what needed to be done for them to become active public speakers, and it was my job to make it happen. Today, aside from my husband, the two of them are my biggest pushers; they push me always to use what they know God has blessed me with, either that or they are just getting back at me for the years I hounded them to speak up and speak out.

Thy word is a lamp unto my feet and a light unto my path.
Psalm 119: 105

The message depicting the excellent news of our Savior lives is a message that must be kept alive. When all other hope is gone, we must cling to the old rugged cross and don't let go. This may be difficult to do from time to time, but just keep praying and keep pushing.

And He gave some to be prophets, evangelists, pastors, and teachers, (12) the

equipping of saints for the work of the ministry, for the edifying of the body of Christ. (13) Until we all come to the unity of the faith, knowledge the Son of God, to be perfect man, to measure the stature of the fullness of Christ.
Ephesians 4:11-13

O give thanks unto the Lord; call upon his name: make known his deeds among the people. **Psalm 105:1**

We never know how God is going to use us to disseminate His message to others, but together we can spread the word of the good news to make a difference. What's keeping you from sharing your story? God is the creator, director, designer, and the publisher of my story; without Him, there would be no story.

Father God, thank You for supplying me with the tools needed to work Your message. Thank You for instructing me on how and where to spread the good news. Help me to stay tuned into You and Your Holy word. Forgive me for the times when I didn't do the things that You told me to do. I pray that Your hands of protection will keep me covered. Please help me to keep my eyes on You. Please send me to where Your message needs to be heard. In Jesus' name, I pray. Amen.

A Stormy Epiphany

DON'T BUILD A LIFE WITHOUT HIM

Chapter Twenty-three

We all like shopping, or at least we like receiving gifts from time to time. When we get rewards from others, we may or may not like what we have received; nevertheless, we should be grateful for the thought of the giver. Christmas time is one of the most popular times of the year for giving gifts. It is a time when lots of people are exchanging gifts with one another. Well, it has also become the most commercialized holiday of the year. The focus on the true meaning of Christmas has been completely lost. The real meaning of Christmas is all about the ultimate gift, and the gift of Jesus Christ as our Savior. God gave His only begotten son so we may live. The ultimate reward is PRICELESS! Jesus paid it all. He paid the price for our sins so we may have a chance to live a life of abundance. I think about the selfless price Jesus paid for me, and my soul cries out, "Thank you, Jesus" for loving me. I've wasted many years and cried many tears, all because I chose not to follow Jesus. While I can't undo the earlier days of my life, I can, and I will make better choices for the remaining days of my life. I have made a choice to work the message in season and out of season. I will work the message when it's welcomed and when it's rejected. I can only do this with Christ at the center of my life. I thank God for seeing something in me I didn't see in myself. He is the all-knowing one, and I will forever be grateful to Him.

For I say, through the grace given unto me, to every man that is among you, not to think of himself more highly than he ought to think; but to think

> *soberly, according as God hath dealt to every man the measure of faith.*
> **Romans 12:3**

None of us can undo the past, but as long as we have breath in our bodies, we can strive to make it right going forward. The world today is full of chaos, prejudices, inequalities, negativity, hatred, greed, and selfishness, which makes the world a lot more challenging to live in. Although we can't escape from these things, we can escape to a place of solace; which is hope, peace, comfort, and protection, found only in the arms of our Savior. In return from our place of solace, we can pray and witness about the blessings found with God. It takes diligence to grow stronger in God and persistence to become the strong, obedient, and humble servant of God. I want to be led by God and follow in His footsteps day by day. The path we follow must be traced by God's hands and governed by His grace.

We see spiritual fruit blossoming in us through the Holy Spirit as we follow Christ and keep His commandments. We no longer are the same. The love of Christ works through us, pouring out to those we encounter. This is evident of a changed life.

> *7 Submit yourselves therefore to God. Resist the devil, and he will flee from you. 8 Draw nigh to God, and he will draw nigh to you. Cleanse your hands, ye sinners; and purify your hearts, ye double minded.*
> **James 4:7-8**

A life with Jesus is the only right *'one size fits all'* deal. Although we all have different needs, and we all grow spiritually at different levels, our Heavenly Father is the only one who can meet the needs of all. No matter what your needs are; how or when you have an obligation, God will supply your need. He specializes in catering to the needs of His people. His specialty is the SURE-FIT. He will work in you until your spiritual growth fits the purpose He has destined for your life. You won't just get in where you fit in, Jesus will make sure you fit in where you are purposed to be in.

Father God, thank You for this life You have given me. Thank You for taking the time to let me know how special I am in your sight. Thank You for seeing in me what others fail to see. I pray that I will always be complementing to others to encourage them and to bring hope to all. Let my light so shine that others desire to be drawn to the light of the world, which is found in Jesus Christ. These and all the blessings I ask in Your precious name. Amen

BLESS IT FORWARD
Chapter Twenty-four

With each year of maturity I am graced with, the more I am inclined to spend time in meditation. There are so many lessons to glean from meditating. The opportunity presents itself with a chance to travel down memory lane. There are perhaps some life events we choose not to remember, but it's ok as long as you don't re-live them. Hindsight is the best view to keep moving forward. Every time you remember where God has brought you from, you will pray for His guidance to keep you moving further away from where you once were. Hindsight also gives you a clear view of the past trials and tribulations you had to experience for your spiritual growth. I surmise you might question the uncomfortable events you encountered just as I did, but it was all a part of our deliverance plan. God's love can deliver us from self-destruction, from being our own worst enemy, from lack of faith, from lack of patience, from unforgiveness, from selfishness, and from all negativity.

31 Let all bitterness, and wrath, and anger, and clamour, and evil speaking, be put away from you, with all malice: 32 And be ye kind one to another, tenderhearted, forgiving one another, even as God for Christ's sake hath forgiven you.
Ephesians 4: 31-32

God is always in complete control, and He knows just what He is doing. God puts our sins behind Him, and He forgets them. He doesn't remind us of our mess-ups, rather He transforms our mess into life changing messages so we might share with the masses

God's power to change.

I often wondered why we keep the sins of others within arm's reach to showcase whenever we feel the urge?

The more we look at the sins of others, the less likely we are to forgive the sinner. Where would we be if God operated this way? Where would we be if God kept our sin in close view and revealed them every time we failed to follow His commandments? Thank God for forgiving and forgetting our sin! I'm so glad God doesn't operate like a man. God's ways are far above our ways, and His thoughts are far above our thoughts. We can rest assured knowing once we ask God to change us, we can forgive others as He forgives us. He will handle the rest. We are now capable of loving others out of the reservoir of love God deposits in the hollow of our hearts. We can also forgive out of that same reservoir God imparts upon us as He forgives us. We cannot do this out of our own power, it is only with the aid of the Lord's power. All things are possible with God.

14 For if ye forgive men their trespasses, your Heavenly Father will also forgive you: 15 But if ye forgive not men their trespasses, neither will your Father forgive your trespasses.
Matthew 6: 14-15

My soul is quickly put into check when I think of the quote by Rubin Carter, *"Hatred. Bitterness, and anger only consume the vessel which contains them. It doesn't hurt another soul."* Most times, when our lives are all caught up in disarray because of things we hold onto, we often lose track of the reason behind the bitterness. This is not only damaging to our physical bodies, but to our mental, spiritual, and psychological bodies as well.

12 Put on therefore, as the elect of God, holy and beloved, bowels of mercies, kindness, humbleness of mind, meekness, longsuffering; 13 Forbearing one another, and forgiving one another, if any man have a quarrel against any: even as Christ forgave you, so also do ye. 14 And above all these things put on charity, which is the bond of perfectness. 15 And let the peace of God rule in your hearts, to the which also ye are called in one body; and be ye thankful.   Colossians 3: 12-15

The sooner we can disconnect from these antics, the sooner we will be able to establish a more palpable relationship with God. The Bible tells us, "It's impossible to please God without faith," well, it's impossible to forgive those who we feel are undeserving without the love of God in our hearts. The heart God resides in must be conducive to loving, forgiving, caring, sharing, and putting others first. God will not reside where chaos lives.

One of the best experiences is giving back. It is always nice to receive and be thought of by family and friends, but it is even more heartwarming to be considered by a stranger. The fact I know what this feels like, motivates me to return the favor to someone unknown to myself. It is natural to give to those whom we love, but it's love that makes us give to those whom we do not know. The blessings we receive from God are not because we have been good or because we deserve them, it's merely because of His love for us. This same love should prompt us to give out of love to those less fortunate than we are. There is nothing more wonderful than grace and mercy which allows us to ***bless it forward***. The more you give, the more He gives to you is true, but our giving should not be out of expectancy, but out of love.

For God is not the author of confusion, but of peace, as in all churches of the saints.   **1 Corinthians 14:33**

God will always do what He says. The Bible said it, and I

believe it. That is all the proof I will ever need. The Bible is a self-authenticating book; it requires no approvals.

> *Heavenly Father, thank You for Your lovingkindness toward me. Thank You for throwing my sins into the sea of forgetfulness and remembering them no more. I pray that You will build me up where I am weak and continue to give me what it takes to forgive others. Please bless those who have a desire to call on Your name but feel unworthy. Help them to realize that we all are unworthy of Your grace and mercy, but You love us despite ourselves. In Jesus' name, I pray. Amen*

DEFINITIVE DIAGNOSIS

Chapter Twenty-five

Most all people, at one time or another have visited a doctor's office. We go to a primary care doctor for diagnosis and treatment. Sometimes we are referred to a specialist if the primary care cannot determine an illness or if it is outside the scope of the doctor's training. A specialist may run a test or perform procedures to determine the issue. Once a diagnosis is obtained, a treatment plan must be put into place.

Well, our spiritual bodies need a checkup as well. This is the time to check in with the spiritual doctor, Dr. Jesus. He has never misdiagnosed or fail to diagnose any of His children. Our spiritual bodies require preventive maintenance, just as our physical bodies do. The check-up with this doctor will eliminate any possibilities of being stricken with a stony heart, He will clean your heart of all impurities. He will mend your broken heart so you will be able to feel and express love again.

Keep thy heart with all diligence; for out of it are the issues of life.
Proverbs 4: 23

A check-up with Jesus will prevent your mind from being stuck in a world of confusion. He is a mind regulator; He will fix your mind to stay on His goodness and grace. The doctor will x-ray your soul and remove all malice so you will feel your brothers' pain. He will repair the hole left in your soul by the careless and unconcern.

A joyful heart is good medicine, but a crushed spirit dries up the bones.
Proverbs 17:22

In other words, this doctor is the master of all doctors. He will be the only doctor you will need for your spiritual healing. Jesus will give you a definitive diagnosis for your spiritual well-being. He will remain with you before, during, and after the diagnosis to see you to the end. When you get sick, and can't get well, just call on the name of Jesus, follow the Great Physician's orders, and rest in his abounding care. He will be at your rescue and deliver you. Not only will you receive a diagnosis complete, but God will provide you a complete healing. Turn to Jesus and be healed. Jesus is the answer for the world today.

Father, God, thank You for being a doctor for my soul. Thank You for being able to see my every need and to heal me in the areas I am in greatest need. Teach me how to listen for Your direction and to be intentional about growing closer to You each day. Please help those who have no desire to seek You. Father God lead me to the places where I can have the most significant impact on Your people. Father continue to be the healer that this world needs. Keep me humble, I pray. Amen.

IRREFUTABLE HEALING

Chapter Twenty-six

Now that we have gotten the proper diagnoses, we must understand the adequate treatment to receive complete healing. It's time to get our prescription filled with the Holy Spirit. We must get to the point in our lives where we are so high on Jesus that nothing or no one will be able to bring us down and keep us down. If you are brought down from your Holy Ghost High, you won't stay down. Although we understand every moment of our lives won't be stress-free, we must realize it's what we do with the stress determines how soon we will be able to get back up. The trust, faith, love, dedication, and devotion we have for God should take us to an immovable spiritual place. We should have no problem getting a refill of the Holy Spirit. God has an endless supply, it's never on backorder. Nothing; absolutely nothing, should be able to separate us from the love of God. This is a separation none of us can afford. Only the love of God will sustain us through all of life's experiences. TRUST HIM! Unlike man, He can never disappoint. Our humanity will get low on life sometimes, but the reality of the love, grace, and mercy of God will not let us stay there. You can get back up again as long as you stay focused, keeping your mind on Jesus.

> ² *Beloved, I wish above all things that thou mayest prosper and be in health, even as thy soul prospereth.*
> **3 John 1:2**

It's like watching a play, then taking an intermission to regroup before taking it to the climax. Life experiences at their lowest points are the intermissions. Be advised to return to the place where the scenes will heighten and take you to a full recovery.

> *2 Bless the Lord, O my soul, and forget not all his benefits: 3 Who forgiveth all thine iniquities; who healeth all thy diseases; 4 Who redeemeth thy life from destruction; who crowneth thee with lovingkindness and tender mercies; 5 Who satisfieth thy mouth with good things; so that thy youth is renewed like the eagle's.*
> **Psalms 103: 2-5**

The end of the show gives you the most meaningful life's experiences called blessings. The ending featuring God Almighty offers you a burst of energy to finish the race. You will get up with exuberant praise on your lips and a song on your heart. Even when you see those in your circle helping you get up, it's all God. God placed these people in your circle because they are chosen to help you build endurance. These circle-mates will help get you where God wants you to be. It's not by chance the people you need are right on time. God has it all worked out in His divine plan. He knows who will reach you and help you and who will not. He has already given them what it will take to contact you. I have personally learned lessons from people whom I least expected. This is because God knows better than I.

You must be open to receive from the experience or the individual whom God chooses. In my finite mind, I can't possibly see what the infinite mind of God sees in others; neither can you. We must trust that God gave everyone something to work with. We must decide how we will use it. Sometimes, we fail to see the message or messenger because we have tunnel vision. We are so focused on what doesn't exist in the immediate, that we overlook the possibilities of the future. When we take the time to observe and analyze our situations with spiritual sight, God will reveal what we cannot comprehend without Him.

My tears of joy flows because of His grace, and I pat my feet in praise and adoration unto Him.

God gives us the ability to build up and protect our personal spaces through His word and grace. The area we live in is our own designated space for eating, sleeping, breathing, loving, learning, and receiving directions. Our space should not be invaded with joy-stealers or blessing-blockers. The more we monitor our space, the more we grow in faith and humility.

The devil comes to run interference against the plans God has for our lives. We must be prepared to block the punts the devil kicks our way. The best defense in preventing the punts is to study the playbook.

The playbook is the Holy Bible. The Bible gives us every play we need to run the race of life and have every victory. God is omniscient, therefore He knows every play. In the game of football, each team watches the other team's film from previous games. This action helps to know how the other side operates and reveal their weaknesses. The devil watches the movie of our lives and use the past experiences to defeat us; to test our offensive line for holes. He studies our failures and uses them to make us bend and eventually fold. He finds what it takes to make us crack under pressure. He looks at your defense to measure the weakness and strengths.

When you think he is coming at you from the left, he will blindside you and come at you from the right. The major thing the enemy fails to recognize is that God wrote the playbook of life, and He is the director of life's film. He knows every trick the devil will throw, and every play he will attempt to run against you to knock you off the righteousness game. God runs the ultimate interference and protects us from possible interceptions. Anything God has His hands on will NEVER fail. Trust and believe He will see you to victory. You will win every time! He won't allow you to experience turnovers and fumble into the hands of the devil.

Lord, thank You for new mercies bestowed upon us each day. Thank You for taking the time to keep us safe in spirit, soul, and body. You've been a way maker and a bridge over trouble waters. Thank you God for running interference on our behalves to keep us protected." Please lead us in the way of righteousness. Your praise will continually be in our mouths. In Jesus' name, Amen.

INTERFERENCE

Chapter Twenty-seven

Life has a way of forcing us to get our lives into perspective. We can do it when the opportunity presents itself, or it will be done for us at some inopportune time. I much rather prefer collecting lessons from every mistake, misfortune, misunderstanding, misrepresentation, or misperception to get on track versus missing out on getting my life in order with God. The risk is much too high, and the price to pay could add up to be astronomical. Jesus has already paid the price for all of our sins; we owe everything to Him. God will run interference to reveal what we are unable to see on our own. We must pray and ask for forgiveness and mean it when we pray so our sins will be forgiven. It is my goal to see the Savior face to face when this life is over. I will praise and worship my Savior in spirit and truth until that day comes. Don't live in this old, cold, unstable, sinful world today and miss out on Heaven tomorrow. We must pray to God before, during, and after trying events in our lives and ask for wisdom and understanding. When we are led by the Holy Spirit, we have what it takes to resist the devil. Just remember, the lower you go for God, the more He will bless you and raise you up for His purpose. This is the opposite of what man does, you go low for man in an attempt to meet them where they are. If you are not careful and prayed up, man will try to keep you low. Every effort you make to get up, man will fight to keep you down. Ask God for discernment to be able to distinguish between those who will lift you up and those who will try to keep you down. Ask God to fill your space with God-fearing, humble spirited, and peacekeeping saints who are excited about building others up. We must learn to protect our areas and time as we wait patiently to hear from God. We must keep our spaces free of negativity, nay-sayers, joy takers, the unmotivated, and the ungrateful. Every time you receive negative energy from those occupying your area, ask God to transform the space and space takers into positive energy.

My life has not been a bed of roses, but I thank God every day for the way He has led me, kept me, comforted me, counseled me, delivered me, changed me, chastised me, forgiven me, but most of all how He loved me! Look to Jesus and be saved. Don't miss Heaven because you chose to serve ONLY the world!

Father God, thank You for everything You have done and for all You continue to do for us. Thank You for loving us enough to care that we not perish. You are so awesome to love us despite ourselves. You keep making ways when it seems all hope is gone. Teach us to be as loving and forgiving as You are. Let your lights so shine through us that others may see a ray of hope and look to You. Help us to spread the love that permeated the hearts of others and spread like wildfire. Keep us looking to You and only You, who is the giver and sustainer of life. In Jesus' name, I pray. Amen

DON'T BE DENIED ETERNITY

Chapter Twenty-eight

The subject of death is an uncomfortable one for most people. It was once that way for me. It was not until I gave my life to Christ that I lost the comfortless notions of death conversations. I now have no fear because a life with Christ means eternal life. God did His work in me. I was able to refrain from looking at the gripping grief of my family members, focus on moving on with my own life. It's all working out in my favor and for the Glory of God.

God indeed works in mysterious ways. However He chooses to maneuver; it shall come to pass. Whenever God is up to something, we can bank on something good happening. Be careful not to allow bad attitudes or negative actions to fuel sin. Make the decision to go in the opposite direction. There is nothing in life worth risking where we will spend eternity.

God has so much love for His children. He sees our every pain and answers our every need. The *"No Child Left Behind Act"* was implemented in an attempt to distribute equality between poor school districts and wealthy ones. Well, the real No Child Left Behind Act was action taken by God from the beginning of time to leave none of His children behind. God wants to see all of His children have life and have it more abundantly. He wants us all to be saved and spend eternity with Him. This act was nothing new, nothing in this world is unique. Harry Truman once said, *"There is nothing new in the world except the history you do not know."*

The thing that hath been, it is that which shall be; and that which is done is that

which shall be done: and there is no new thing under the sun.
Ecclesiastes 1:9

You see, there isn't anything that God doesn't know, haven't seen, or haven't done. He is the all and all! I can't begin to thank God for all the opportunities in life that He has afforded me. Let us not forget where God has brought us, and we will remember to thank Him in advance for where He is taking us. We have to juggle life, let it run its course, maneuver the unexpected, and still maintain some sense of normalcy. I need God's help with every bit of life experience.

Jesus states,

27 My sheep hear my voice, and I know them, and they follow me: 28 And I give unto them eternal life; and they shall never perish, neither shall any man pluck them out of my hand.
John 10: 27-28

And the world passeth away, and the lust thereof: but he that doeth the will of God abideth forever.
1 John 2: 17

God is busy at work in our lives every day, even when we don't recognize it. You may be allowed to go through some uncomfortable circumstances, but it is all a part of God's plan and purpose for your life. When things don't seem to work out, don't be discouraged. Remember, the more patience you display, the more your trust in God is being demonstrated. God is actively orchestrating situations in our lives to put us in place to receive His blessings. Once we receive His benefits, He will place us in a space where we have the opportunity to bless and serve others. Bless It Forward!

The trials, tribulations, and downfalls only reveal to us how incomplete and helpless we are without Him. Our most valuable growth takes place during our trials and tribulations. These acts of misfortunes move our hearts to seek God.

You may be dealing with thorns in your flesh such as thorns of disappointment, loneliness, heartache, depression, but God will give you the grace needed to make it through any situation you may face. While thorns are uncomfortable, they do help you grow closer to your purpose and more dependent on God. It would be so easy for God to remove these thorns, but that would interrupt His plan from being carried out.

For the wages of sin is death; but the gift of God is eternal life through Jesus Christ our Lord.
Romans 6: 23

Our brokenness allows us to see the areas we have not surrendered to Him. We should humble ourselves to God and ask for help in submitting our all in all to Him.

10 Therefore I take pleasure in infirmities, in reproaches, in necessities, in persecutions, in distresses for Christ's sake: for when I am weak, then am I strong.
2 Corinthians 12:10

We are crushed and broken to be made into vessels meet for the Master's use. Only He can make us whole. The discomforts in our lives will eventually break us of our resistance to lean totally on the Lord. Just as a loving mother or father disciplines a child to correct them, God allows discipline in our lives through trials and tribulations to fix us. He loves us so much, this I do know! He wants to see each of us reach our full potential in Him. The more we train ourselves to focus on God and not our surroundings, the closer we will grow to Him, and the more we can handle our circumstances spiritually.

I reminisce when my kids were very young, and I took them for swimming lessons. My son, Mikeem, had no fear and caught on very quickly, learning to swim like a fish. My daughter was fearful, and her lessons were postponed until she became older. Whenever we went on vacations after our son's successful swimming lessons, my husband and I would notice how our son would take his sister by the hand and try to assure her that she was safe as he assisted her with swimming. Our son knew that his sister would be comfortable with him, and most of all, she trusted him. That's the kind of comfortability God desires us to have in Him. He will take you by the hand and lead you to a place of safety. We should feel safe going to God and putting our complete trust in Him. God's love, presence, and protection for us should not require some irrefutable proof before we become believers. The fact that you have survived the storms in your life should be proof enough.

³² Now therefore hearken unto me, O ye children: for blessed are they that keep my ways. ³³ Hear instruction, and be wise, and refuse it not. ³⁴ Blessed is the man that heareth me, watching daily at my gates, waiting at the posts of my doors. ³⁵ For whoso findeth me findeth life, and shall obtain favour of the Lord. ³⁶ But he that sinneth against me wrongeth his own soul: all they that hate me love death.
Proverbs 8:32

God works through all sorts of avenues, with different kinds of people, and many types of experiences to get us where He wants us to be. The Bible tells us that the angel of the Lord appeared to

Moses in a burning bush; we never know how or who He will use to get our attention. He may use something or someone who we least expect to give us instructions and directions. We must be willing to put in time to evaluate situations to know what God is trying to tell us through the burning bushes He places in our view.

> Lord, thank You for holding my hand and leading me to where You want me to be. Thank You for not leaving me or giving up on me when I didn't always do right. You are my all and all, and, in all things, I give You the praise. Please bless those that are less fortunate and help me be sensitive to the needs of others. Teach me Your ways all the days of my life, and I will be so careful to give only You honor and praise. In Jesus' name, I pray. Amen

Before life ends on this side, we all will experience some good days and some bad days. Hopefully, your good days will outweigh your bad days. As for me, I refuse to complain, because my good days certainly exceed my bad days! When I look back over my life, I know that I can never live to deserve all that God has blessed me with. I love life and what God has allowed me to experience on my journey, and for that, I just want to praise Him. There is no place I would rather be than in the space that I currently occupy.

God stepped in at the lowest point of my storm; the point where I was drowning. I was reminded of the disciples when they were up against the storm in the boat, and Jesus had fallen asleep. The disciples were experiencing fear of drowning. Jesus asked the disciples upon awakening, "Where is your faith?" I, too, needed to be rescued from my storm. I could imagine Jesus asking me that same question when I was in the midst of my storm. The disciples already witnessed what Jesus was capable of, and so had I, but for some strange reason, it was as if Jesus was sleeping this one out. Little did I know, He was right by my side handling my storm the whole time. He sheltered my soul when the winds blew fiercely. He covered my mental state when the raining drenched my mind. He fed my soul from the spiritual realm of His Holy Spirit. He protected my body with the power of His might to keep me alive. My Heavenly Father was working when I knew it and when I knew not. I could hear my Father say on that morning of my "STORMY EPIPHANY," "Ye of little faith," you can lean on me, and I won't let you down. God knows how much it will take to get each of us to the point of non-wavering faith. It took the storms of death to get me to a place where I trusted God completely and totally, no matter how dim things looked. We must learn to accept that God will come, but it's all in His time and His way. He knows precisely when HIS appearance will have the most significant impact on building our faith. That's why HE is God all by Himself. It behooves us to prayerfully ask God to help us analyze every life storm through our spiritual eyes and not our physical eyes. The physical eye will analyze with blinders on, but through the spiritual eye, you will see what God is revealing. He will show you that greater things are on the horizon after the storm.

[9] *But as it is written, Eye hath not seen, nor ear heard, neither have entered into the heart of man, the things which God hath prepared for them that love him.*
1 Corinthians 2:9

It is a continual work getting where God wants us to be. In the meantime, we must be sowing seeds of love, mercy, forgiveness, compassion, empathy, sharing, and caring for those we meet throughout life.

I have come to realize that every step of my journey was necessary to cover ground needed to acclimate me to the purpose for my life. There will still be difficult moments to face from time to time, but I thank God I know He will be with me every step of the way. We must stay on the battlefield for the Lord and work His message of eternal life every chance we get. When this life is over, it is my desire to hear my Master say WELL DONE, what is it that you desire?

Father God, I come as humble as I know how thanking You for all You have allowed me to do. Thank You for who You have created me to be. You said in Your word that if we humble ourselves before You, You will lift us up. I pray that You will clothe my heart, mind, body, and soul with humility. Keep us all in a safe place and protect us from all evil, especially the evil that is self-inflicted. Grant us thy peace that we may work Your message in the areas where it is needed the most. Let us not forget from where You brought us by Your grace and Your mercy. Teach us to love and forgive our brothers and sisters as You forgive us. Father God, if it is Your will, please bring peace to this dying world. We will be so careful to give You all the glory, all the honor, and all the praise. In Jesus' name, we pray. Amen

IN THE STILL

When our movements are made still, we behold the beauty created by God's holy hands

When our voices are made still, the voice of reason is hushed, and the voice of peace arise

As distractions are made still, noise of yesterday and tomorrow will soon vanish

As we listen closely to today and give attention to its value

When we debunk the thoughts of being self-reliant, we realize our capacities are finite

We are drawn to look above and call on the one with whom wisdom is infinite

When we are still, we can examine our full life story

Remembering how God worked it out for our benefit and to His glory

When we are still enough to notice the chirping of the birds as they sing

We are appalled at the sound of sweet music that they bring

When we are in still places, we can take in the smell of the rain
We begin to lose ourselves, in the thoughts that the showers bring

As hearts and spirits are made to be still, we quickly feel our neighbors' pain

For in our service to others, indeed more blessings we gain

When our minds are still, we think of reaching out to each other

Embracing every opportunity to lean on one another

In places of stillness, we take time to inhale the gentle breeze

Something so simple, yet so often missed

When our grace is placed in stillness, we can begin to count our blessings

As we examine each one of them, we realized they were laced with love

When we are admonished for being in a state of hurries, our world is made to be still

We are directed to reset our priorities to line up with God's divine will

When plans and purposes are made to be still, we re-evaluate our efforts

When our lives are made to be still, we collect and dissect our inner-most thoughts.

We are moved to praise God, thanking Him that all hope is not lost

When the world is made to be still, clear direction can be sought

As we gain a sense of purpose, we find it divinely driven, as it ought

For in the midst of all stillness, great things are found, great things will evolve

Our purpose in the world as we once viewed, will have definitive meaning to its' resolve.

Debra Q. Rogers 2020

ABOUT THE AUTHOR

Debra Q Rogers was born January 28, 1961 and is a native of South Carolina. She is a published author and poet, a devoted wife, mother of two, and grandmother of one. Debra is an avid reader and writer and has been since early childhood. She has always anticipated writing a book. Debra has a heart for those who have been cast aside or simply ignored. Debra's favorite pass times are serving in the local schools' reading programs and assisting at hospice facilities. Debra finds that she receives her greatest joy when helping someone along the way. If she encourages at least one person each day, then she is moving in the right direction. She believes God places us in environments to help others. Debra serves as a Notary Public for the state of South Carolina.

Rogers works diligently in mentoring, motivating, and encouraging others. Her favorite Bible verses are Philippians 2:2-4 (NIV) and Proverbs 12:25 (AMP).

Debra is a member of the Pen of a Ready Writer Society and continues to embrace the beauty of bringing words to life thru writing. Debra's love and passion for God and to serve others in need is her motivation for life.

www.ingramcontent.com/pod-product-compliance
Lightning Source LLC
Chambersburg PA
CBHW071408290426
44108CB00014B/1734